Delights
&Disciplines
of Bible Study

Delights
&Disciplines
of Bible Study

Warren W.
Wiersbe

David C Cook®
transforming lives together

DELIGHTS AND DISCIPLINES OF BIBLE STUDY
Published by David C Cook
4050 Lee Vance Drive
Colorado Springs, CO 80918 U.S.A.

David C Cook U.K., Kingsway Communications
Eastbourne, East Sussex BN23 6NT, England

The graphic circle C logo is a registered trademark of David C Cook.

LCCN 2017942196
ISBN 978-1-4347-1056-7
eISBN 978-0-8307-7211-7

© 2018 Warren W. Wiersbe
The Team: Matt Lockhart, Lindsay Black, Keith Jones, Amy
Konyndyk, Stephanie Bennett, Susan Murdock
Cover Design: James Hershberger
Cover Photo: Getty Images

Printed in the United States of America

First Edition 2018

1 2 3 4 5 6 7 8 9 10

102517

Contents

Introduction

The purpose of this book is to help you find enlightenment and enjoyment as you study the Word of God. Don't think of these chapters as a lecture series. Please see them as conversations between you and me about growing "in the grace and knowledge of our Lord and Savior Jesus Christ" (2 Pet. 3:18). I'll offer some ideas about many passages in the Bible, and your job is to take those ideas and run with them. Weigh what I say with the Scriptures, and use what I say as a beginning of your own exploration of the Bible.

You should know that this book is about the practical use of hermeneutics, a word adapted from a Greek word meaning "skilled in interpretation." Whether we are reading Shakespeare, the daily newspaper, or the Bible, we must follow recognized principles of interpretation or we will misunderstand what we are studying. Every believer needs to know how to interpret the Bible accurately and to apply its truths practically in daily life.

Let me assure you that I have written this book for sheep and lambs and not for giraffes! You shouldn't have to stretch too high to grasp what you want. H. A. Ironside, one of my pastoral predecessors at the Moody Church in Chicago, used to say, "I try to put the cookies on the lowest shelf so that everybody can reach them." Believe me, he didn't just try—he succeeded! His expositions of the Scriptures still reach the minds and hearts of serious Bible students.

As you read this book, please have your Bible at hand so you can look up and read the verses that are cited but not quoted. The goal of hermeneutics is to help serious Bible students interpret the Scriptures accurately so they can apply divine truth practically and detect false teachings. We must be determined, with God's help, to become like the person described in Psalm 1:2 whose "delight is in the law of the Lord, and in His law he meditates day and night." Or like Ezra the scribe who "prepared his heart to seek the law of the Lord, and to do it, and to teach statues and ordinances in Israel" (Ezra 7:10). (See also Ps. 119:97–104.)

The material shared in this book is written for any Christian who wants to go deeper in personal Bible study as well as for those who study the Bible while preparing to teach individuals or classes or to preach to congregations. A better understanding of the Bible will enrich your life in many ways, so go for it! Bible study should be an adventure and not an affliction. If it is a burden, something is wrong in the heart. I hope this book will help you develop a sense of the excitement of studying the Bible.

One more thing: if you have never memorized the books of the Bible in sequence, please do so. One of the marks of serious Bible students is their ability to find the texts they are seeking. You won't need to buy cumbersome page markers or keep consulting the table of contents. If you really want to be a successful Bible student, take the time to learn the books of the Bible.

May the Lord bless all of us as we seek to understand His precious Word! May the holy Word of God humble us, encourage us, and enable us to serve the Lord in the power of the Holy Spirit!

Warren W. Wiersbe

Chapter 1

Why Study the Bible?

Since there are so many good books to read these days, both classical and contemporary, why should we take the time to read and study an ancient book like the Bible? A bestseller for years, it has been translated into many languages and is available in a variety of editions, but it is still an ancient book about ancient peoples that was written in three ancient languages—Hebrew, Aramaic, and Greek. Many people respect the Bible but don't read it, and many who do read it don't always understand it. Further, those who do understand it don't always obey it as they should.

Why should we study the Bible? We know that God commands us to study His Word (2 Tim. 2:15), and we know we must obey that command, but there are other reasons. I've listed several of them below, but note this is not an exhaustive list and that these are not noted in order of importance.

We Should Study the Bible Because of What the Bible Is

Let's look at some of the word pictures that describe the Bible in the Bible. The Bible is compared to *gold* and *honey.* "The fear of the LORD is clean, enduring forever; the judgments of the LORD are true and righteous altogether. More to be desired are they than gold, yea than much fine gold; sweeter also than honey and the honeycomb" (Ps. 19:9–10; see also Ps. 119:103). The Lord said to the prophet Jeremiah, "Is not My word like fire … and like a hammer that breaks the rock in pieces?" (Jer. 23:29).

The Bible is like *a lamp*: "Your word is a lamp to my feet and a light to my path" (Ps. 119:105; and see also v. 130 and 2 Pet. 1:19). The Bible is like *food* for the inner person. It is milk (1 Cor. 3:1–3; Heb. 5:11–13; 1 Pet. 2:2), solid food (Heb. 5:11–14), bread (Matt. 4:4; Deut. 8:3), and honey (Ps. 19:9–10).

God's Word is also a *mirror* (James 1:23–25). This is a very important metaphor that I will say more about later. In His parable of the sower, Jesus compared the Word to *seed* (Matt. 13:1–9, 18–33). Paul wrote about the cleansing power of the "*water* by the word" (Eph. 5:25–26), a metaphor Jesus also used in the upper room (John 13:10; 15:3). Keep in mind that water for washing represents the Word of God, while water for drinking represents the Spirit of God (John 7:37–38). The Word of God is also a *sword* (Eph. 6:17 and Heb. 4:12). In fact, when the people heard Peter preach at Pentecost, they were "cut to the heart" by the Word of God (Acts 2:37).

I will introduce other metaphors and similes in chapter 8, but this selection should at least whet your appetite. The Bible is rich in metaphors and similes that convey precious truths that we need to know. Understanding biblical imagery is one of the keys to accurate interpretation.

We Should Study the Bible Because of What the Bible Does

I was leisurely browsing through the stacks in our seminary library one afternoon and picked up a magazine that looked interesting. I turned the pages and was suddenly arrested by this:

----

2 Timothy 3:16–17

All Scripture is given by inspiration
of God, and is profitable
for doctrine—that's what is right;
for reproof—that's what is not right;
for correction—that's how to get right;
for instruction in righteousness—
that's how to stay right;
that the man of God may be
perfect, throughly furnished
unto all good works (KJV).

The word perfect means "complete" or "adequately prepared," and "throughly," of course, means "thoroughly." Ponder those verses until they become a part of your inner person. This is what true Bible study is all about. Life is transformed when God's Word is in control.

In those few words in 2 Timothy 3:16–17, Paul told young Timothy how to treat the inspired Word of God. I don't know of any other summary that states so clearly the goals of Bible study. If studying the Scriptures teaches me sound doctrine, convicts me of what is wrong in my life, and shows me how to correct my errors and not repeat them, then I want to be a good student of the inspired Word of God. Our personal goal is spiritual maturity, being adequately equipped by the Lord to serve Him as the Holy Spirit enables us to know and to do the will of God. We want to glorify Him and minister to others as the Lord directs. Many self-help books line the shelves today, but none of them can claim to be inspired by the God of the universe as is the Bible, nor can they claim to be inerrant, living, and powerful (Heb. 4:12).

The Bible is actually a library of books, each written at a different time about different matters, but all of them focus on Jesus Christ, the Son of God, and the nation of Israel that gave us the Bible and the Savior of the world. As we read in the Gospels, "Salvation is of the Jews" (John 4:22), meaning it came through them. Knowing their story and how God worked among them is essential. The Bible not only gives us history, biography, and prophecy but also poetry, wisdom, promises, warnings, and practical counsel. Perhaps the best way to introduce you to the wonders of God's Word is to list some of the metaphors *used to describe* the Bible found *in* the Bible. In case you have forgotten, let me remind you that a metaphor is a figure of speech that uses one thing to define or illustrate another thing. For example, "That office is a circus" or "Their marriage is a merry-go-round" are metaphors. A simile, one type of metaphor to watch for, uses the words *like* or *as*. "Our vacation was like a civil war" or "That guy is as slippery as an eel" would be classified as similes.

We Should Study the Bible Because the Bible Exalts Jesus Christ

The major theme of the Bible is Jesus Christ, the Son of God and the Savior of the world. We must never forget that *the way we treat the Bible is the way we treat Jesus Christ.* Jesus is the *incarnate* Word of God (John 1:1–14) and the Bible is the *inspired* written Word of God (2 Tim. 3:16–17), and you cannot separate the two. Let me show how they go together.

The Bible is the holy Word of God, "which He promised before through His prophets in the Holy Scriptures" (Rom. 1:2). Jesus is the holy Son of God, "that Holy One who is to be born will be called the Son of God" (Luke 1:35). Now, get your Bible and look up the references that follow:

- Jesus is the Light of the World (John 8:12), and the Scriptures are a light to guide us in this world (Ps. 119:105, 130, 133; 2 Pet. 1:19).
- Jesus is Life (John 11:25; 14:6), and the Word of God is life (Heb. 4:12 ; Phil. 2:16).
- Jesus is the eternal Son of God (John 1:1–2), and the Bible is the eternal Word of God (Ps. 119:89, 152, 160).
- Jesus is righteous (2 Tim. 4:8; 1 John 2:1) and the Bible is righteous (Ps. 119:7, 106, 160; Rom. 7:12).

- Jesus is the Truth (John 14:6), and the Bible is truth (Ps. 119:43; Eph. 1:13).
- Loving and obeying Jesus (John 15:9–10) involves loving and obeying the Word of God (Ps. 119:47–48, 97, 127, 150).
- Delighting ourselves in the Word of God is also to delight ourselves in the Son of God as the Word was with God and was God (John 1:1; Ps. 1:2; 112:1; 1 John 1:4).

I could expand this list, but I'm sure you get the point: the way we treat the Bible is the way we treat Jesus Christ. If we ignore the Bible, we are ignoring Jesus. If we read and understand God's Word but don't obey it, we are disobeying Jesus. On the other hand, to love God's Word, learn it, and live it means to love our Lord, know Him better, and introduce Him to others more readily. Just as Jesus counseled His disciples, so the Bible counsels us as we are guided by the Holy Spirit (John 16:12–15; Ps. 119:24, 169; 2 Tim. 3:14–17).

We Should Study the Bible Because Knowing the Bible Strengthens Our Spiritual Life

Prayer and the Word of God must always go together. The prophet Samuel prayed for the people and taught them the Scriptures (1 Sam. 12:23–24). The apostles said, "But we will give ourselves continually to prayer and to the ministry of the word" (Acts 6:4); and Jesus promised, "If you abide in Me, and My words abide in you, you will ask what you desire, and it shall be done for you" (John 15:7). King David wrote in Psalm 37:4, "Delight yourself also in the Lord, and He shall give you the desires of your heart." The Word of God teaches us how to pray and what to pray for; otherwise, we risk praying in vain. We read the Bible, meditate on its truths, and obey its commands not because we want to debate people about religion or show off what we think we know but because we love Jesus and want to be more and more like Him.

How important is your Bible in your life? It should be more important than food (Job 23:12; Jer. 15:16; Matt. 4:1–4). Do you value the riches of God's Word more than material riches? They were more valuable to the person who wrote Psalm 119 (see vv. 72, 127). Is spending time in the Word of God more important to you than "sleeping in" or taking a nap? The psalmist put the Scriptures ahead of sleep (119:55, 62, 148, and 63:6). Peter, James, and John went to sleep on the Mount of Transfiguration and also in Gethsemane where Jesus was praying (Luke 9:28–36; Matt. 26:36–46). Our Lord asks us as He asked them, "Could you not watch with Me one hour?" (v. 40).

If we sincerely desire to become more effective Bible students and therefore more effective servants of the Lord, we must have the right priorities; and one of the first priorities is to set aside uninterrupted time for studying the Word of God. It isn't enough just to read the Word of God, meditate on it, and pray, as important as those disciplines are. We must learn to compare Scripture with Scripture and trust God's Spirit to teach us the deeper truths that are there. We must delight in God's Word and say with the psalmist, "Your word is a lamp to my feet and a light to my path" (Ps. 119:105). The heart of every problem is the problem in the heart.

We Should Study the Bible Because the Enemy Knows the Bible

When Jesus faced Satan's temptations, He overcame him by using the Scriptures (Matt. 4:1–11). *But Satan also quoted the Scripture!* Read Psalm 91:11–12 and Matthew 4:5–6. Satan quoted the verses, but Jesus deflected each of the Evil One's quotes with another verse. The Bible does not contradict itself, but the truths found in the Bible must be kept in balance. Jesus said to Satan, "It is written again …" (Matt. 4:7). One of my seminary professors used to remind the class that "a text out of context is a pretext," and he was right. It's so important that we see the whole picture and not just a snapshot here and there.

Satan is identified with darkness (Luke 22:53), but the Bible with light (Ps. 119:105). Satan is a liar and a murderer (John 8:44), but the Bible is truth and life (Ps. 119:43; Phil. 2:14–16). Obeying Satan leads to bondage, but obeying God's Word leads to freedom (John 8:30–36). The believer's duty and privilege is to walk in the light and have fellowship with God (1 John 1:5–7) in order to stay in the light and avoid Satan's attempts to steer us into darkness. There is no darkness in heaven (Rev. 21:23), and there is no light in hell, for hell is outer darkness.

We Should Study the Bible Because Knowing the Bible Even Helps Our General Education

This is not the most important benefit of Bible study, but it is still worth knowing. Familiarity with the Bible is like taking a college course on the art, music, literature, and laws of Western civilization.

For example, the novel *Moby-Dick* by Herman Melville opens with "Call me Ishmael." The reader who has never read Genesis 16 and 17 is not likely to know the significance of this sentence, but the alert Bible student will grasp its meaning immediately. One summer, I read *Moby-Dick* again and marked the biblical quotations and allusions in it, and I was amazed at how many there were. What is true of literature is also true of music. Not to know our Lord's pains in Gethsemane is to miss much of the riches of the *St. Matthew Passion* by J. S. Bach. Biblical allusions and quotations saturate classical Christian worship music. I wonder how many worshippers are confused by the second verse of "Come Thou Fount," which begins "Here I raise my Ebenezer"? It's based on 1 Samuel 7:12, where the prophet Samuel set up a monument and called it "Ebenezer—stone of help." If you are fortunate to worship at a church that sings the great hymns of the faith, your knowledge of Scripture will make your worship much more meaningful.

What I'm saying is simply this: a rich Bible knowledge not only enriches us spiritually (if we obey what it commands) but also enables us to appreciate and understand the classical productions of the Western world. I recall strolling through an art gallery in London and thanking God for blessing me with training in the Bible. Some of those paintings would have been puzzles to me were it not for what I had learned in confirmation class, seminary, and my own personal studies.

The secret to fulfilling any responsibility in life is simply turning work into joy because of our love for our Master. At least eight times in Psalm 119, the psalmist announces his delights in God's Word (vv. 16, 24, 35, 47, 70, 77, 92, 174). To this list, you can add Psalms

1:2; 19:8; and 112:1. When we delight in the Word of God and rejoice at what the Spirit teaches us, our relationship with the Bible means blessings and not burdens. An increasing working knowledge of Scripture changes our lives and enables us to serve others to the glory of God. Not to study the Bible ourselves means going without spiritual food and having to be spoon fed by others. Shame on us! It also means we accumulate the defilement of the world and desperately need a good shower or bath! Not to study God's Word means a static relationship with the Lord, and that grieves the Spirit of God who longs to instruct us and mature us in the Christian life. This book emphasizes *studying* the Bible, not just reading it devotionally, as important as that is.

Believers who depend only on others for their nourishment and enlightenment miss the joy of adventuring with their Bibles, and that even applies to you as you read this book. It's my privilege to help you discover several Bible study principles, and it's your privilege to put those principles into practice and experience adventures with your Bible. The Lord wants us to imitate the prophet Jeremiah, who wrote, "Your words were found, and I ate them, and Your word was to me the joy and rejoicing of my heart; for I am called by Your name, O Lord God of hosts" (15:16).

ADVENTURE ASSIGNMENT #1

It's time to ask yourself, *What is my motive for wanting to study the Bible seriously, and am I ready to pay the price?* Why do you want to go deeper? Do you want to impress people with your Bible knowledge? That's a poor basis. Do you want to draw nearer to the Lord and become more like Him? Do you have a weakness you want to overcome? Whatever your reason, be sure it pleases the Lord and that your maturing in Christ will bring Him glory. "Search me, O God, and know my heart; try me, and know my anxieties; and see if there is any wicked way in me, and lead me in the way everlasting" (Ps. 139:23–24).

Chapter 2

Are You Ready for Serious Bible Study?

Our personal daily devotional time is very important, but it may not be the equivalent of serious Bible study. We need both. Reading the Bible systematically in a devotional way can teach us basic Bible history and doctrine, and as we meditate and pray, we "abide in Christ" (John 15:1–17). We express our love for the Lord, we worship Him, and we pray for ourselves and others. The Lord prepares and equips us for the day before us so that we can face it courageously and live victoriously. But there is more.

Personal Bible study also should be regular and systematic, but it is not necessarily done every day, except perhaps by pastors and teachers who minister to others. When I was in the pastorate and also teaching ministerial students, I maintained a strict study schedule that was bolstered by my daily devotional time—and there were times when the two beautifully blended. Your devotional time is like eating a daily meal, while serious Bible study is like visiting the health club and exercising. We can read the Bible devotionally, but we also need to study it doctrinally, historically, and thematically. We need to see what each book in the Bible says and how it relates to the other books. We need to study the Word of God in depth so that we may know what is right, what is not right, how to get right, and how to stay right. In our daily devotional time, we rarely use other books to help us understand the Bible, except perhaps a daily devotional guide, while serious students consult basic books that are like keys that open the doors to deeper Bible knowledge. Our goal in all this is to grow toward maturity. Read Hebrews 5:12–14.

Those Who Are Born Again

The first requirement for successful Bible study is personal faith in Jesus Christ, your Savior and Lord: "But the natural [unsaved] man does not receive the things of the Spirit of God, for they are foolishness to him; nor can he know them, because they are spiritually discerned" (1 Cor. 2:14). John chapter 3 introduces us to Nicodemus, "the teacher of Israel" (v. 10) who could not understand how to be born again. He came to Jesus at night and proved that he was "in the dark" spiritually. But he listened to what Jesus taught him, and eventually he was born again (John 19:38–42).

Please understand that unbelievers *ought* to read the Bible—especially John's gospel—and take it to heart; but until the Holy Spirit begins to work, their understanding is limited. Their reading is usually routine and not seriously penetrating, but as the Lord works, He may open their eyes and hearts and bring them to saving faith. During my years of ministry, I have heard unconverted religious people teach "Bible lessons" or preach sermons, and I have also read some of their books. Their ignorance of basic spiritual truth has shocked me. They were spiritually dead, and the dead cannot see.

This current age we live in is not only secular in its thinking and teaching, but it is definitely anti-Christian in its living and in its attitude toward the Christian faith. Those immersed in it tolerate Christians but do everything they can to oppose them and their message. That is why we must study the Bible and "be prepared to give an answer" to those who ask about our faith (1 Pet. 3:15 NIV).

Those Who Take the Time Needed for Serious Study

A second requirement is a willingness to devote time to reading, studying, and digesting what the Lord teaches you. I will be giving you "adventure assignments" as we move through the book, and I trust you will take them seriously. The noted British preacher Dr. G. Campbell Morgan would read a book of the Bible fifty times before he attempted to analyze it and write his exposition commentary. Fifty times! All of us claim to be busy, but if we are too busy to allow the Holy Spirit to teach us how to live and serve, then we are *too* busy. I know professed Christians who can recite endless facts about politics or sports or TV personalities, but they can't find the Ten Commandments or the Beatitudes in their Bible.

The older I get, the more I realize how precious time is, and I do my best not to waste it or allow others to waste it for me. When we study God's Word, we are not *spending* time; we are *investing* time in that which counts for eternity. When believers get to heaven, they take with them their knowledge of the Scriptures. All of us will have new bodies like our Lord's glorious body, but we will not automatically know everything about the Bible. Will there be classes to help us catch up? I don't know, but I do know there is a great deal yet for me to discover in that wonderful book we call the Bible! I have been studying God's Word seriously since 1945, have written expositions on every book of the Bible, and have taught many of them verse by verse, yet I know how much more I need to learn. I have been privileged to know and to hear gifted Bible teachers and have learned from them, but they have also challenged me to dig deeper and learn more.

Please evaluate your schedule and make time for serious Bible study. Pray these words with David: "But as for me, I trust in You, O Lord; I say, 'You are my God.' My times are in Your hand" (Ps. 31:14–15).

Those Who Live in the Spirit

A third essential is faith in the Holy Spirit, your teacher, and obedience to His will. I have often wished I could sit down with authors whose books I have read and have them explain the things I didn't really understand. Imagine how much more I could learn! We have the blessed Holy Spirit dwelling within us, *and He wrote the Bible* (see 2 Tim. 3:16 and 2 Pet. 1:19–21). When I was a lost sinner, I claimed John 3:16, and the Lord saved me. Can I not claim John 14:26 and be taught by the Holy Spirit? In that passage, Jesus said, "But the helper, the Holy Spirit, whom the Father will send in My name, He will teach you all things, and bring to your remembrance all things that I said to you."

The Spirit sometimes teaches us personally, but at other times, He uses books or Christian teachers. I don't know how many times the Lord has awakened me at night and started teaching from passages I had pondered the day before. I prefer to attend day school, but if the teacher wants to enroll me in night school, I am willing to learn. I keep a small lamp on my nightstand, right next to a pen and pad of paper, and I write down what I have learned; if I don't write it down, it will be forgotten by morning!

I read about a famous philosopher who awakened one night and had an overwhelming insight. He wrote it down and went cheerfully back to sleep. The next morning, he remembered the experience, picked up the piece of paper, and read: "Everything in the world is a manifestation of turpentine." I have never had that kind of experience, but I can show you notes that were written at night and still made sense! My point is simply this: let the Spirit of God teach you when He pleases and the way He pleases. I confess that I have sometimes left the "table," where a feast of God's Word lay before me, to jot down thoughts the Lord has graciously given me. Keep in mind that we must "take in" spiritual seeds through our studies before they can bear fruit. The Holy Spirit does not work in a vacuum.

Prayer is an essential Spirit-led ministry in the Christian life, for prayer and study go together: "If any of you lacks wisdom, let him ask of God, who gives to all liberally and without reproach, and it will be given to him" (James 1:5). Note the prayers in Psalm 119. On many occasions, I have struggled with making a satisfying meal out of a Bible passage and a stack of notes, and I have paused for prayer. Then I would either remain at my desk and wait or leave my desk and go look out the window, and the Lord would show me my errors and the best way to correct them. Then I would bow and give thanks. I carry note cards and a pen in my wallet so that even when I'm away from my desk, I can still write down what the Lord teaches me, no matter where I am. I imagine most of you have a smart phone that you find convenient for reading the Bible and taking notes. Use it!

Those Who Have an Inquiring Mind

My fourth essential for serious Bible students may seem strange to you, but here it goes: we must have an open and inquisitive mind as well as patience as we study. Back in 1966, a drunken driver going eighty miles an hour hit my car head on, and only God's grace and a seat belt saved my life. As I lay in bed, first in the intensive care ward and then in my own room, I pondered the event and asked the Lord what He was seeking to teach me. The only other time I had been a patient in a hospital was when I had my tonsils taken out, and I was there only one day. I wasn't even born in the hospital! I was born at home. Being a hospital patient was a new experience for me.

While confined to bed, Bible promises began to come to my mind; as I read my Bible, new truths captured me and I wondered how long they had been there! Charles Haddon Spurgeon said that the promises of God never shine brighter than in the furnace of affliction, and he was right. When I was released and eventually returned to my ministry, you can be sure that I had much more compassion when I visited people in the hospital. I knew better what to say and how to pray for the patients, and I also knew when to keep quiet—and when to leave! They didn't teach me those important facts in five years of seminary, but, thank God, I finally learned them. If we open God's Word, the Spirit can open our eyes and hearts to teach us—through life's difficult experiences, its joyful events, and even its routine happenings. The important thing is to abide in Christ, pray, meditate, and listen to what God is saying to you. I want to be like those two Emmaus disciples and have fellowship with the Lord, a flame in my heart, and a message on my tongue to tell others (Luke 24:13–35). Cold-hearted saints are complainers and critics, not witnesses.

Those Who Ask the Right Questions

Technicians of any sort must ask the right questions if they hope to discover the problems to address and provide the right solutions, and so must Bible students as they seek to understand a Scripture passage. Here are some simple questions I have used for many years, and I recommend them to you.

The first question is this: *What is the major theme of this passage?* The Bible is a profoundly rich book, and we can learn many things from one passage; therefore, we must be careful to focus first on the major themes. One Christmas Sunday, I heard a preacher announce Matthew 2:1–12 as his text—the visit of the magi to the baby Jesus—and he proceeded to preach a sermon on tithing. Although the magi gave gifts and we are to tithe our gifts, the larger story has nothing to do with tithing; I did not catch the connection.

Let's look at Psalm 23, a familiar passage in which David used the image of sheep and shepherds to describe the Lord's care for His own people, which is the major theme of the psalm. This image was certainly meaningful to the Jewish people in David's day, but how much does it mean to city folks today? I never saw a flock of sheep until I was in third grade and our teacher arranged for the class to be bussed to a beautiful farm outside the city. The farmer explained shepherding to us and answered our questions, and from that day on, Psalm 23 made sense to me. Psalm 23 is brief and its theme is clear, but what about a passage like Ephesians 1:1–14? It is not a psalm, but it could well have been used as a worship hymn in the early church. The word blessed introduces the passage (v. 3) and appears to be the key word. God's people have been blessed by the triune God—the Father (vv. 3–6), the Son (vv. 7–12), and the Holy Spirit (vv. 13–14).

In the Old Testament and the four Gospels, you find many narrative passages that are more difficult to tie down. Our Lord's parable of the persistent widow (Luke 18:1–8) seems, on the surface, to urge us to pester God and wear Him out with our prayers until we get what we want, but just the opposite is true. Our Lord is not comparing; He is contrasting. The parable is saying, "If an unconcerned, selfish judge finally meets the needs of a poor, persistent widow, how much more would your loving heavenly Father meet the needs of His precious children when they ask Him?" God is not like the judge, for He is patient and generous, and the church is not like the widow, for God encourages us to ask, and He promises to meet our needs. Prayer is not pestering our Father. It is claiming His promises, fellowshipping with Him in love, and telling Him what we need.

The second question is this: *How is this theme presented?* Is the passage a parable, a poem or song, a doctrinal exposition, a prophecy, a personal narrative, or a slice of history? The possibilities are challenging. You don't treat a parable as you would a psalm, nor do you read a narrative as you would a prayer. The apostle Paul's message to the Ephesian elders (Acts 20:17–38) is really a farewell sermon that brought everybody to tears. His review of his ministry in Ephesus is actually a short course in pastoral work! Hidden in the Greek text are at least ten pictures of his ministry that teach us what our privileges and responsibilities are today. I once used this passage as the basis for a series of addresses at a Bible college and then repeated them over the Back to the Bible radio ministry. Mary's song in Luke 1:46–56 is another rich passage, and it shows that she knew her Old Testament! Jesus' prayer in John 17 is saturated with practical theology that every believer needs to know and practice.

Question three: *What does the passage mean to the original listeners or readers?* The ancient Near East and the Roman Empire were radically different from our rapidly-changing world today, although human nature was pretty much the same. We can't read very far into the Bible before we encounter envy, murder, lying, drunkenness, and indecency. Things were so bad that the Lord had to send a flood that wiped out everybody except Noah and his family. In contrast, the nation of Israel trembled at Mt. Sinai (Exod. 19—24) when God gave His laws, yet people today read or recite the Ten Commandments as casually as if they were a grocery list. How did the churches Paul planted react to his letters? Did the churches in Galatia repent of their legalism, and did the Corinthian church send Paul their promised donation for the Jewish believers in the Holy Land? Did Philemon welcome and forgive his runaway slave when he came home?

Question four: *What does the passage mean to me personally?* We not only study the Bible but the Bible studies us! One morning, I was working on a sermon from James 4, and I realized I had to phone an acquaintance and straighten out a misunderstanding. James had warned me, and I had to obey. Once I did, my studies went much better. The Word of God is a mirror that reveals what God sees when He looks into us. If I don't apply the text first to myself, I can't expect the Lord to help me prepare messages that He can bless. If what I'm preparing doesn't bless my own heart, it's not likely to bless others.

Question five: *How can I make the passage meaningful to others?* Our Lord was a master at telling stories that touched people right where they lived. He also knew how to quote the Old Testament Scriptures. Even the hard-hearted Pharisees knew when He was talking to them. In order to answer this final question, you and I must know both the Word of God and the people to whom we are speaking. An unhappy church member said, "Our pastor is invisible during the week and incomprehensible on Sunday." Whether you are a preacher or a Sunday school teacher or a youth sponsor, you need to know that people look to you for encouragement. This doesn't mean we carry secrets into the pulpit, but it does mean we carry the burdens and battles of the people on our hearts and seek to give encouragement. From the first words of the introduction to the final "amen," we must speak the truth in love (Eph. 4:15). If we do, the Lord will open up opportunities for personal conversations that you can use to bring wisdom and spiritual growth to troubled believers.

Those Who Obey What
God Teaches Them

We do not study the Bible so we can debate and display our knowledge, though we must be able to defend the faith (1 Pet. 3:15). We rob ourselves of blessings and rob God of glory when we know God's will but don't obey. Build your "life house" on the sand by not putting God's Word into action, and the next storm will destroy it (Matt. 7:24–27). "But be doers of the word, and not hearers only, deceiving yourselves" (James 1:22). "Now by this we know that we know Him, if we keep His commandments" (1 John 2:3). "If you keep My commandments, you will abide in My love, just as I have kept My Father's commandments and abide in His love" (John 15:10). Claim the "he shall know" promise of John 7:17.

Those Who Seek to Glorify God and
Become More Like the Master

This goal needs no elaboration.

ADVENTURE ASSIGNMENT #2

Set aside time to read Genesis 1 four or five times. As you read, take notes on the facts and truths that the Lord gives you. Keep in mind the questions given in this chapter.

Chapter 3

The Tools Available

If we were to mine for gold, build a house, or prepare a meal, we would need adequate tools to do the work successfully, and the same principle applies to Bible study. To be sure, the Holy Spirit teaches us, *but the Spirit does not work in a vacuum.* The Word of God is seed (Luke 8:11), and it must be planted in the heart and watered with prayer and meditation if the Spirit is to cause it to bear fruit. Over the years, I have gathered together a book collection to assist me in my adventures with my Bible. These include …

A Bible

Select a Bible that suits you. My first choice is *The New American Standard Bible*, the cloth-bound library edition. It is an accurate translation and features wide margins for your notes as well as an excellent system of cross-references. Do not mark your Bible with a ballpoint pen or a fountain pen, but use a fine-point pen with acid-free ink. (You can find these pens wherever art supplies are sold.) They are perfect for underlining key words and phrases, connecting verses, and jotting notes in the margins. You may have a favorite Bible for your devotional reading, but this will be your "study Bible."

Speaking of study Bibles, I advise you not to use one for your own Bible study. There is no space for notes, and the pages are filled with material. I have fourteen different study Bibles in my library and make good use of them, but when I'm doing my own personal studying, I use my faithful *NASB*. In a sense, I'm writing my own study Bible!

A Good Concordance

Next, select a good complete concordance, one that has a number system that gives you access to both Hebrew and Greek dictionaries. You look up the word you are studying, find the verse (or verses) it is in, and look up the number next to the verse. This leads you to the original Hebrew or Greek word. *The New American Standard Exhaustive Concordance of the Bible* (Holman Publishers) and *The NIV Exhaustive Concordance* (Zondervan) are both designed this way. *The New Strong's Exhaustive Concordance of the Bible* is a similar volume, geared to the King James Version of the Bible. It also has a "Key Verse Comparison Chart" that gives you access to five other translations. If you are only trying to find a verse, the familiar *Cruden's Complete Concordance* may do the job, but real Bible study goes beyond the beloved King James Version.

My own preference is *The New NIV Exhaustive Concordance* because it uses the number system also found in two other valuable Zondervan concordances: *The Hebrew English Concordance to the Old*

Testament and *The Greek English Concordance to the New Testament.* Please don't let these titles frighten you! I studied both Greek and Hebrew in seminary but must confess that I lack a mastery of these languages and depend on these three books to assist me. The same Hebrew or Greek word may be translated into any number of English words in the same book of the Bible, and the careful student will want to be able to identify them. For example, in the NIV gospel of Luke, the Greek word *charis* is translated into five different English words: *grace, gracious, favor, thank,* and *credit.* The number system is easy to use and helps us become more accurate in our exegesis, or interpretation of the text. Frankly, I use several concordances, including Mr. Cruden's classic mentioned above. It includes several word lists that have saved me time and trouble!

Some Other Helpful Books

This leads me to mention a volume that has been around since 1940: *The Expository Dictionary of New Testament Words* by W. E. Vine (Revell). It is rich in content and a joy to read. The author explains the meanings of Greek words and how similar words differ. You do not need to know Greek to use and enjoy this book. I highly recommend it to you.

Secure a good Bible dictionary and/or Bible encyclopedia. *The New Unger Bible Dictionary* (Moody Press) and *The New International Dictionary of the Bible* (Zondervan) are both on my shelf and are often consulted. The four volumes of *The International Standard Bible Encyclopedia* (Eerdmans) are a treasury of information for the inquiring student.

I have saved one of my favorite tools for last: *The New Treasury of Scripture Knowledge*, edited by Jerome H. Smith and published in 1992 by Thomas Nelson. This book gives you thousands of cross-references for every book in the Bible. "The best commentary on the Bible is the Bible itself," R. A. Torrey used to say, and he was right. The original *Treasury* was based on the cross-references found in *The Scott Bible*, a commentary by Thomas Scott, a British Episcopal rector. The set I own was published in Philadelphia in 1872. The new Nelson edition is a masterpiece of editorial skill as the editor has corrected errors found in the older editions and added considerably more material and helpful notes. *If you are not using this book, you are robbing yourself of a valuable biblical resource!*

Be Encouraged!

Careful and successful workers always use the best tools, but please don't sell your car to get funds to purchase the books I have suggested. The blessing of serious Bible study depends primarily on our surrender to the Holy Spirit, our walk with the Lord, our careful reading of the text, and our obedience to what God shows us. But as I mentioned before, the Holy Spirit does not work in a vacuum, and He can use the tools I have suggested to teach us valuable spiritual truths. The Lord has given teachers to the church, and many of these teachers have shared their discoveries in the books they have compiled or written, and we are foolish not to allow them to teach us today. It requires time and sacrifice for anyone to build a basic library, but it is worth it. The psalmist wrote, "The law of Your mouth is better to me than thousands of coins of gold and silver" (Ps. 119:72). Strive to be a careful and successful worker to the glory of God.

ADVENTURE ASSIGNMENT #3

I suggest you carry with you, perhaps in your purse or wallet, the names of the books in the brief bibliography given in this chapter. You never know when you might discover one of these valuable books at a very low price—or as a gift with no price at all! Follow postings for sales of used books, and also watch the book catalogs. You would be surprised how few people know the value of these books to serious students.

Chapter 4

The Pentateuch

Genesis to Deuteronomy

The thirty-nine books of the Old Testament focus predominantly on the people of Israel—their battles and blessings, their leaders, and, most of all, their responsibility as a nation to obey the Lord and bring the promised Redeemer into the world. The word *Pentateuch* means "five tools" in Greek, and the term describes the first five books of the Bible, without which we would not fully understand the rest of the Bible.

Genesis: The Lord Forms a Family

Genesis describes the creation of the universe, the creation of the human race, and the beginnings of the Jewish people who gave us Jesus and the Bible. "For He spoke, and it was done; He commanded, and it stood fast" (Ps. 33:9). God built Abraham and Sarah's family as it grew from one son, Isaac, into the twelve tribes of Israel. Four men stand out in Genesis: Abraham, Isaac, Jacob, and Joseph. Each man had his weaknesses and disappointments, but the Lord used all of them to accomplish His will.

As you read Genesis, you will note that the Lord was not in a hurry. He could have spoken the universe into being with one word, but He took six days. He could have given Abraham and Sarah a son when they were much younger, but He waited twenty-five years. To serve God effectively, we must practice Psalm 37:7—"Rest in the Lord, and wait patiently for Him; Do not fret because of him who prospers in his way, because of the man who brings wicked schemes to pass." Also note that God's will involved believing women as well as obedient men. God worked in and through families as well as individuals.

Eve disobeyed God and shared the fruit of the tree of life with her husband (Gen. 3), but Adam's disobedience plunged the entire human race into sin and judgment; for Satan deceived Eve, but Adam sinned with his eyes wide open (see 2 Cor. 11:3; 1 Tim. 2:14). Romans 5 is Paul's explanation of our fall, and note in that chapter the repetition of the word reign.

Genesis 3:15 is the first mention in Scripture of the coming Redeemer, and verse 21 is the first mention of slaying an animal to provide covering for guilty sinners. The offering of Isaac (Gen. 22) points us to Jesus and the cross, the only begotten Son obeying the will of the Father.

Abraham and Sarah's pilgrim life is of utmost importance, for the people God blesses and uses have always "walk[ed] by faith, not by sight" (2 Cor. 5:7). To walk by faith means to obey the Lord no matter our feelings, our circumstances, or our consequences. Wherever Abraham and Sarah went, they identified the spot with a tent and an altar. Open your Bible and, beginning at Genesis 12:8, trace Abraham's pilgrimage and look for the tent and the altar. The tent tells us they were pilgrims and strangers in the land, and the altar testifies to their faith in the living God. Together, they served as a testimony to all the pagan peoples around them. We believers today are pilgrims (1 Pet. 2:11), because we don't belong to this world system and we live in "tents" (our bodies—2 Cor. 5:1, 4) until we receive our eternal home in heaven.

Exodus: The Lord Builds a Nation

Exodus is Greek for "road out," and the book by that name tells us how the Lord delivered the Jewish people from the bondage of Egypt and formed them into a nation. Moses and his brother Aaron led the people. The judgments the Lord sent against Egypt revealed their gods' and goddesses' inability to protect Pharaoh and his people. At Mt. Sinai, the Lord gave Moses the laws that governed the nation. The Jews had been slaves in Egypt for hundreds of years (Acts 7:6), and Moses didn't have an easy time turning a nation of slaves into the people of God. More than once, the people wanted to rebel and return to Egypt, where they at least had security and were cared for by their Egyptian masters. The Lord wanted them to be free and to walk by faith, but they had a difficult time learning their lessons.

Events and imagery that help us better understand the Redeemer and the redemption that He purchased on the cross saturate the Pentateuch. The Passover (Feast of Unleavened Bread) is one of the most important (Exod. 11—13). The lamb in the Passover meal, of course, represents the Lord Jesus Christ (John 1:29, 36; Isa. 53:7;

Acts 8:32, 1 Pet. 1:19). I especially like the sequence in Exodus 12: "a lamb" (v. 3), "the lamb" (v. 4), "your lamb" (v. 5). Another sequence enriches me. Isaac asked Abraham his father, "Where is the lamb …?" (Gen. 22:7), and John the Baptist gave the answer: "Behold! The Lamb of God who takes away the sin of the world!" (John 1:29). One day, we shall join the heavenly choir and praise Jesus, saying, "Worthy is the Lamb who was slain …" (Rev. 5:12). As you read God's Word, note these interesting sequences.

The Jewish nation did not understand the meaning of freedom. At Mt. Sinai, Moses presented to the nation the laws God gave them so that in obeying them they would mature and enjoy true freedom. The British theologian P. T. Forsyth wrote in *Positive Preaching and the Modern Mind*, "The first duty of every soul is to find not its freedom but its Master."[1] Jesus said, "And you shall know the truth, and the truth shall make you free" (John 8:32). True freedom is not doing whatever we want to do but doing whatever the Lord wants us to do. To be bound by the freedom of God's law and God's love is to be freed from the bondage of sin and selfishness.

Leviticus: The Lord Sets a Standard: "Be Holy as I Am Holy"

Leviticus records the ministry of the Levites, the family Levi founded and who served first at the tabernacle and then in the temple built by Solomon. The emphasis in Leviticus is on holiness and obedience to the laws God established at Sinai. Both Exodus and Leviticus focus on personal holiness: "For I am the Lord your God. You shall therefore consecrate yourselves, and you shall be holy; for I am holy" (Lev. 11:44; see also 11:4–45; 19:2; 20:7, 26; Deut. 14:2). The apostle Peter applied this commandment to all Christians (1 Pet. 1:15–16).

Leviticus 13 and 14, two of the longest chapters in the book, deal with leprosy, a disease that was to the ancient world what cancer is to our modern world. Why did the Spirit of God devote so much space to a disease that today is not a menace? Because in Scripture, leprosy is a picture of sin, and the cleansing of the leper is a picture of salvation. Note how often the word *unclean* is used in these two chapters. It means "ceremonially unclean," unfit to be in the camp. Like sin, leprosy is "deeper than the skin" (13:3), it spreads (vv. 6–8), it defiles and destroys fellowship (vv. 45–46), and it is fit for the fire (v. 55), *but the leper can be cleansed and so may lost sinners*! "Lord, if You are willing, You can make me clean," a leper said to Jesus; and He replied, "I am willing; be cleansed." Jesus touched him! The man was instantly healed (see Matt. 8:1–4)!

Leviticus chapter 14 describes the ceremony that restored the leper to fellowship in the camp. The leper did not go to the priest; the priest went to the leper outside the camp. Note the parallel with Jesus: "for the Son of man has come to seek and to save that which was lost" (Luke 19:10). Two birds were used in the cleansing ceremony in Leviticus. Priests shed one bird's blood inside a clay jar, and the other was dipped into that blood and freed to fly away. A lamb was slain and the blood applied to the right ear, thumb, and big toe of the leper. Studying the books of the Old Testament prepares us for our studies of the New Testament books.

One of the delights of Old Testament Bible study is discovering how the New Testament writers quoted the Old Testament and shed light on prophecies, promises, and events. When Israel walked by faith and obeyed God, they enjoyed His blessings and testified to the idolatrous nations around them; but whenever they disobeyed, they were defeated and lost God's blessing. Instead of trusting the Lord for their needs, they asked Him to give them a king, and that was the beginning of trouble. Their first king was Saul, a giant in physical stature but stunted in spiritual understanding. He was followed by David, whose faith in God brought victory and peace to the land. Alas, some of David's sons ignored their father's example and broke God's commandments and their father's heart. His son Solomon brought prosperity to the nation, but his son Rehoboam listened to his young friends instead of the experienced elders and divided the nation. More than just to predict future events, the Lord raised up prophets to proclaim God's truth and call the people from their idols and back to the Lord. Many of their kings disobeyed, and when they did, the nation as a whole suffered. Ultimately, the Assyrians conquered the northern kingdom (Israel) and Babylon conquered the southern kingdom (Judah).

We must remember that Israel is the Lord's chosen people, set apart to accomplish His purposes on earth, especially the writing of the Scriptures and giving birth to the promised Messiah. Whenever the people rebelled against the Lord and deliberately sinned, they not only grieved their Lord but they also jeopardized their divinely given ministries on earth. From the time of Abraham and Sarah until Jesus finished His work on earth and ascended to heaven, there was always a faithful Jewish remnant. Today, a remnant of believing Jews and Gentiles that faithfully serves the Lord remains (Rom. 11:5).

Numbers: The Lord Disciplines His People for Their Unbelief

The book of Numbers contains many statistics, as the name suggests. It records complaints as the twelve tribes marched through the wilderness to the Promised Land. If the Israelites had focused on their future blessings instead of looking back on their so-called "security" in Egypt, they would have obeyed Moses and been filled with joy. It has well been said that the "good old days" are a combination of a bad memory and a good imagination. In the book of Leviticus, the Lord manifests long-suffering toward His people and remains always faithful to His grumbling, unbelieving people. Occasionally, He chastened them, and they repented, but they were inclined to maximize life in Egypt and minimize the Lord's blessings.

Numbers, which I mentioned is well-named, also contains the census of the people as they approached the Promised Land and got equipped for battle. But all was not well because the people tended to complain and criticize Moses and Aaron and blame them for their trials. The Lord was testing the people and teaching them how to live by faith. I have often said that a faith that can't be tested can't be trusted.

When they arrived at Kadesh Barnea, the doorway into Canaan, instead of trusting God for guidance and victory, the people sent twelve men to "spy out the land" that God had prepared for them. The men came back, and ten of them shared a tale of woe that discouraged everybody—except Moses, Aaron, two spies, Caleb and Joshua. The people would have stoned Moses had the Lord not intervened. Instead of entering Canaan by faith and claiming their

God-given inheritance, the people wandered in the wilderness until
that entire unbelieving generation had died—except for the four
men I mentioned. It took eleven days to travel from Mount Horeb
(Sinai) to Kadesh Barnea (Deut. 1:2), but the people's unbelief and
rebellion turned it into forty years!

What does all this mean to us today? For one thing, it encourages us to walk by faith and trust the Lord to see us through. If we
are walking by faith, obeying His commandments always leads to
His enablements. How does the Lord increase our faith? He teaches
us from His Word (Rom. 10:17) and tests us with difficult circumstances. Again, a faith that can't be tested can't be trusted, and the
Israelites resisted being tested. There were giants in Canaan, so big
that the Israelites were only grasshoppers! "How often the Israelites
provoked Him in the wilderness, and grieved Him in the desert!
Yes, again and again they tempted God, and limited the Holy One
of Israel" (Ps. 78:40–41).

Every Christian, church, and parachurch ministry must be tested
if they are to glorify the Lord by claiming by faith the inheritance He
has planned for them. I have pastored three churches, two of which
experienced building programs, and I have also served on the staffs of
two parachurch ministries. In all five of these ministries, God tested
us in various ways. How easy it seemed for some people to complain to God and fear moving ahead by faith. But the leadership and
enough of the others involved were convinced that God would give
us His help. They prayed and believed, and God blessed and gave us
victory. In my first pastorate, an elderly couple were great encourag-
ers to my wife and me. They told me one day, "Every church comes
to a Kadesh Barnea place in its ministry and is tested to step out by

faith and go forward. If they stand still, they will go backward and miss the blessings God wants them to have." I took that to heart and God saw us through. "And this is the victory that has overcome the world—our faith" (1 John 5:4).

Deuteronomy: The Lord Gives His Nation a New Beginning

It's unfortunate that some of our gifted Christian poets and song-writers have used Canaan, the Promised Land, as a type or picture of heaven because, while turning people's eyes toward heaven is essential, heaven is not what the Promised Land stands for in the Christian life. It's obvious that we are not going to fight wars and kill people in heaven as Israel did in Canaan, or make mistakes as Joshua did, or deliberately disobey the Lord as Achan did. The book of Hebrews makes it clear that the Promised Land is a type of the spiritual inheritance believers have by faith *today* as they walk with God and obey His will. God's children have a spiritual inheritance *today* from which they may draw as they live the Christian life and do the Father's will. Except for Moses, Joshua, and Caleb, the Jews who were delivered from Egypt all died during their journey after the nation refused to enter Canaan in Kadesh Barnea.

Deuteronomy means "second law." At Sinai, the law had been given to the generation delivered from Egypt, but that generation died off during the nation's march to Canaan. The new generation would conquer the enemy and take possession of the Promised Land, and they needed to understand God's law. Moses reviewed the history of the forty years' march of the nation and announced the law to the new generation before they entered the land (Deut. 1:1–8). After God's people had entered the land and captured some cities, Joshua led them in renewing their covenant with the Lord (Josh. 8:30–35). Now the nation of pilgrims would become a nation of settlers, but they would not succeed unless they obeyed God's law. Alas, they did not always honor the Lord and obey His law, and the Lord had to discipline them. Over the centuries, many of their people—including priests and kings—turned to idols and imitated the godless nations around them. But there are professed Christians today who love the world and drift back into the old life (Phil. 3:17–21), so let's begin with our own needs today.

Moses gave God's truth to the new generation of Israelites as they prepared to enter the Promised Land and claim their inheritance. They would be pilgrims no more but would become settlers, and Moses told them plainly how to behave. He briefly reviewed the history of their pilgrimage from Egypt to Canaan and what the Lord had done for them. He also warned them not to imitate the nations around them, a warning they refused to heed. The Israelites began to imitate the idolatrous nations around them. They asked for a king. They worshipped idols. They neglected their spiritual responsibilities. They forgot how the Lord had blessed them, and they failed to worship Him as the law demanded.

It was important that Israel maintain faith in the Lord and obedience to the Lord, for Israel was to provide the nations of the world with the Word of God and the Savior, Jesus Christ. "Salvation is of the Jews" (John 4:22). The devil used idolatry, immorality, and intermarriage with the pagans to defile the nation, but a faithful believing remnant always remained dedicated to the Lord, just as there is today. We must learn from the past if we are to be obedient in the present and prepared for the future. The Lord has a wonderful future planned for His people if they will trust Him and obey Him.

The Scottish preacher Alexander Whyte defined the victorious Christian life as "a series of new beginnings." We all have our weaknesses and failures, but we can always make a new beginning as we feed on the Word of God, pray, and seek to serve the Lord. Satan reminds us of our defeats because he wants us to be discouraged, but our Father wants to encourage us to repent and return. "Through the Lord's mercies we are not consumed, because His compassions fail not. They are new every morning; great is Your faithfulness" (Lam. 3:22–23). No matter how much we may have failed yesterday, we can confess our sins, be forgiven, and start afresh (1 John 1:9).

It's worth noting that Jesus quoted three times from Deuteronomy when the devil tempted Him (Matt. 4:1–11). Matthew 4:4 is from Deuteronomy 8:3, Matthew 4:7 is from Deuteronomy 6:16, and Matthew 4:10 is from Deuteronomy 6:13. These quotations not only reveal our Lord's knowledge of Scripture, but they also show His insight into the meaning of Scripture. How many of us would know those verses from Deuteronomy and apply them as He did? The Pentateuch contains a rich mine of spiritual truth, and may the Holy Spirit help us dig deeper!

Four words pretty much summarize Deuteronomy's message: *hear* (used twenty-four times), *learn, keep,* and *do.* Together they describe *obedience* (see 11:13–14; 4:40; 12:28; and 29:9). Churches today need to understand the importance of teaching the younger generation what the Christian life and the church are all about. The older saints must challenge the new generations to learn from them and to prepare themselves to take the places of the veterans when God calls them home. Older pastors and teachers must mentor the younger pastors and teachers and encourage them to serve. Each local church is one generation short of extinction, so let's follow Moses' example and equip the younger generation for places of leadership (see Ps. 48:12–14; 71:17–18; and 78:1–8).

ADVENTURE ASSIGNMENT #4

Genesis 49 records Jacob's last words as he spoke to his sons before his death. Read it several times and ponder how you would have felt if you had been the child this father was speaking to. What does Jacob teach us about human nature? What images in the chapter point to Jesus?

Chapter 5

Conquest, Confusion, and Compassion

Joshua, Judges, and Ruth

Joshua is the book of victory as the Israelites obey Joshua and Joshua obeys God. Each tribe receives its inheritance and settles down to enjoy the land of milk and honey. But Joshua dies and a new generation arrives and begins to imitate the idolatrous nations around them. The Lord raises up judges who seek to bring the people back to the Lord and defeat their enemies. The book of Ruth is a beautiful love story that builds a bridge to David, the ancestor of Messiah. Each book different but with one major theme: the Lord is God and His people must obey Him from their hearts.

Conquest: The Book of Joshua, the Book of Conquered Kings

Many poets and lyricists have used Israel's crossing of the Jordan River and entering Canaan as a picture of Christians dying and going to heaven. Such art has long encouraged hurting readers and listeners to look to the hope of heaven in a profound and meaningful way. During trials, heaven is sometimes exactly where our eyes should turn. However, there are weaknesses to the analogy that are important for serious Bible scholars to understand, even if they continue to cherish much about the songs and poems. One song says, "I don't want to cross Jordan alone,"[1] and another says, "On Jordan's stormy banks I stand / And cast a wistful eye / To Canaan's fair and happy land / Where my possessions lie."[2] Surely there will be no armies or warfare in heaven like there was in Canaan! No, the account of Israel crossing the Jordan and taking possession of the land God promised them pictures believers *today* claiming their spiritual inheritance in Christ *today* and experiencing a victorious Christ-life *today.* The book of Hebrews, chapters 3 and 4, uses the conquest of Canaan to instruct believers today on how to claim their spiritual riches in Christ. If we don't, we will end up wandering through life as a generation of Jews did back in the days of Moses.

In many ways, the book of Joshua shows him as an excellent example of a confident, capable leader.

God uses leaders who begin as servants. Joshua is called Moses' "assistant" in Exodus 24:13 and his "servant" in Exodus 33:11. His given name was Oshea or Hoshea, and Moses changed it to Joshua (Num. 13:8, 16). It means "the Lord saves" or "the Lord is salvation."

After the Israelites' exodus from Egypt, the Amalekites attacked them, so Moses appointed Joshua to lead the army and Joshua won the battle (Exod. 17:8–16). It's a basic biblical principle that if we want to become leaders, we must first be servants (see Num. 11:28; Matt. 25:21, 23). The Chinese Christian leader Watchman Nee wrote, "Not until we take the place of a servant can He take His place as Lord."[3] David was a servant long before he became the king, and Jesus told His disciples, "I am among you as the One who serves" (Luke 22:27).

God uses leaders who seek His will and obey it, starting in their own homes. In his farewell address to the nation, Joshua said, "As for me and my house, we will serve the Lᴏʀᴅ" (Josh. 24:15). If we cannot be spiritual leaders in our own household, how can we lead in the house of God (1 Tim. 3:5)? It is unfortunate that some of the tribal leaders in Israel did not fully obey the Lord and failed to remove the pagan inhabitants from the land as God had commanded them (see Num. 21:1–3; Deut. 20; Judg. 3:1–7). Like yeast spreading in a lump of dough, the enemy's sins spread through a nation and lead to disobedience and defilement (see 2 Cor. 6:14–18).

God uses leaders who put others first. Joshua had the privilege of helping assign the inheritances to the tribes of Israel, and yet he received his inheritance last (Josh. 19:49–51). Paul may have had Joshua in mind when he wrote Philippians 2:3—"in lowliness of mind let each esteem others better than himself." Some versions read "more important than himself." True leaders know how to sacrifice for the sake of others.

God uses leaders who acknowledge their mistakes and seek to correct them. Joshua assumed that the city of Ai was easy to conquer, but he did not pause to consult the Lord and was defeated. When he humbled himself before the Lord, Joshua heard from God that there was a traitor in the ranks, and it was Achan. Once the traitor was judged, Israel went on to victory (Josh. 7—8). Deceived by the Gibeonites' lies, Joshua made a treaty with them, which was against the Lord's law (ch. 9). Joshua kept his word but made the deceptive Gibeonites slaves to the Israelites. How easy it is to walk by sight instead of by faith! Had Joshua taken time to pray instead of examining the "evidence," the Lord would have guided him and revealed that these "visitors" were neighbors and enemies. It pays to wait upon the Lord and seek His guidance instead of jumping to conclusions on the basis of deceptive "evidence."

The nineteenth-century British preacher F. W. Robertson said, "Life, like war, is a series of mistakes, and he is not the best Christian nor the best general who makes the fewest false steps … but he is the best who wins the most splendid victories by the retrieval of mistakes. Forget mistakes; organize victory out of mistakes."[4]

God uses leaders who are themselves and not imitators of others. During my many years of ministry, I have followed some great men of dedication and achievement, but I have never tried to imitate their leadership style. If the Holy Spirit and I were to work together, I had to be myself—my *best* self—and seek to glorify the Lord. Joshua was Moses' successor but not his imitator. Joshua was a military man while Moses was a liberator, legislator, and an organizer. At different times, ministries need different leaders in order to meet different needs, and search committees must keep this in mind. Each of us is unique and can make different contributions to the work of the Lord.

God uses leaders who are disciplined. "Then Joshua rose early in the morning …" (Josh. 3:1). Our Lord rose to pray early in the morning (Mark 1:35), and Abraham rose early to do God's will, difficult as it was (Gen. 22:3). David was an early riser (Ps. 5:3). Early in my Christian life, I learned to get up early and spend time reading the Word of God, meditating, and praying, whether I was at home, in a motel room, or in a plane headed overseas. To meet God in the morning is to have God with you all the day. To leave Him behind is to face the day alone, and that is dangerous.

God uses leaders who explain and encourage. It's not enough to tell God's people what they are to do; they also must understand why they are doing it. As I read the book of Joshua, I get the impression that Joshua encouraged his people and kept them informed. As our Lord made His way up to Jerusalem that final week, He told the disciples what would happen. They didn't fully understand His plans, but they knew He was doing the Father's will. Be an encourager!

Some people dislike and even criticize the military language used in Scripture and in hymnals, but whether we like it or not, God's people have enemies and must fight battles. "Fight the good fight of faith," Paul admonished Timothy (1 Tim. 6:12), and he commanded the saints in Ephesus to "put on the whole armor of God" (Eph. 6:11). There are political issues today that are actually religious matters that affect our basic freedoms, and if we are not ready for the battle, we will be defeated. The devil and his hosts are organized against us, and we must be awake, armed, and alert. *Every Christian is important and must answer "Here" to the roll call.* The apostle John tells us that "God is love" (1 John 4:8), but we also know that Moses sang, "The LORD is a man of war; the LORD is His name" (Exod. 15:3).

Confusion: The Book of Judges, the Book of "No King"

A new generation of Israelites had taken possession of the Promised Land, a generation that had never experienced the slavery of Egypt or the challenges of a long wilderness march. They took over the inheritance assigned to them and settled down to enjoy the "land of milk and honey." They did not kill or expel all of the former idolatrous inhabitants as God had commanded them (Deut. 7:1–11; Ps. 106:34–39) and soon became interested in their neighbors' activities, including their godless religion. God's people began to "sample" some of their religious practices, all of which the laws of the Lord God prohibited; and the nation gradually abandoned God's instructions. "In those days there was no king in Israel; everyone did what was right in his own eyes" (Judg. 17:6, and see 18:1; 19:1; 21:25; and Deut. 12:8).

"What's right for you may not be right for me," said a college student. "There are no absolutes." "Does that include the statement you just made?" his friend asked. "It sounds pretty absolute to me." That ended the conversation.

Though they had not been there personally, the Jewish people knew what had happened at Mt. Sinai—the thunder and lightning, the revelation of God's glory, God's voice from heaven, and the declaration of God's commandments to His people. When the nation's spiritual life began to decay, the Lord chastened His people as Moses, in his farewell address to the nation, said He would (Deut. 13). The Lord had called Israel to be His special people, and He had made it clear they were not to imitate the wicked practices of the pagan nations around them. When they did, He brought other nations to invade them and put them under bondage. The people would then repent of their sins, return to the Lord, and the Lord would raise up "judges" to drive out the enemy and set His people free (see Judg. 2:11–23). The Holy Spirit would empower the judges to awaken the people and lead them in defeating their enemies. It's worth noting that, by His Spirit, the Lord empowered only the judge (see Judg. 3:10; 6:34; 11:29; 14:16, 19; and 15:14), while in Acts 2, the Spirit filled all of God's people. As the people of God who have the Holy Spirit, let's focus on Acts 1:8 and make a difference in this world!

It is interesting to see the various "weapons" that were used during the time of the judges: a dagger (3:16); an ox goad (3:31); a tent peg (4:21); torches, pitchers, and trumpets (7:16–25); a millstone (9:53); and the jawbone of a donkey (15:15). Neither the weapon nor the warrior gave the victory but the power of the God of Israel.

Why was it so important that the people of Israel remain obedient to the Lord and separated from the practices of the godless nations? Because "salvation is of the Jews" (John 4:22). The Jewish people would witness to the world of the one true and living God. They would also give the lost world the Holy Scriptures and the Savior, Jesus Christ. This they could not do unless they were separated from the deceptive and destructive religious beliefs and practices of other nations. This same principle applies to the church today: "Do not be unequally yoked together with unbelievers" (2 Cor. 6:14). To love the world and imitate it is to lose our love for the Father and the blessings that He shares with us (1 John 2:15–17).

The nation of Israel asked for a king so they could be like the other nations and fight off their enemies (1 Sam. 8). Where was their faith in the Lord? Could a human leader do for the nation what God had already done? The more the church becomes like the world, the less influence it will have on the world, and our witness will be ineffective. We grieve the Holy Spirit when we compromise with the world, and He removes His power from us. You meet all sorts of people as you study the judges in this book. Some abused the office by putting themselves ahead of their ministry while others were faithful to the Lord and His people. Keep in mind that the judges did not rule over the entire nation as would a king but primarily over different tribes and areas.

Samson, one of these judges, had great strength when the enemy tested him, but he was very weak when the ladies tempted him. He was raised in a godly home, given great physical strength, and handed an opportunity to lead the nation to victory, but his life ended in shame. He played with sin, and it robbed him of power. Judges 16:21 describes the blinding effects of sin, the binding effects of sin, and the grinding effects of sin. It wasn't worth it! Samson went from the dynamics of conquest to the disgrace of captivity. Yes, he gave his life to defeat the enemy, but it would have been better had he given his life fully to the Lord and done the will of God.

In a sense, we are living in the times of the judges today, for "doing your own thing in your own way" is the most popular way of life for young and old. George MacDonald called this philosophy of life "respectable selfishness."[5] The late star Lucille Ball said, "I have an everyday religion that works for me. Love yourself first, and everything else falls into line."[6] People who live only for themselves inevitably get tired of the company they keep and miss out on what Jesus called "abundant life" (see John 10:10).

Compassion: The Book of Ruth, God Is King

It's remarkable that the events in this beautiful story occurred "in the days when the judges ruled" (Ruth 1:1)! Yes, the book opens with a famine and three funerals, but it closes with a wedding and the birth of an ancestor of King David (Ruth 4:17–22). Ruth is named in Jesus' genealogy (Matt. 1:5), which is quite an honor for a widow from the land of Moab: "An Ammonite or Moabite shall not enter the assembly of the LORD; even to the tenth generation" (Deut. 23:3). But Ruth got in! All of this tells us that the worst of times may turn out to become the best of times when we trust God and depend on His grace. This love story encourages us not to give up but to obey the Lord and trust Him to work things out. Romans 8:28 had not been written yet, but the truth that "all things work together for good to those who love God" is certainly demonstrated in the life of Ruth the Moabite.

There was no king in Israel, but there was a King in heaven, and Ruth trusted that King as her own Lord and Savior (Ruth 1:15–18). In spite of three painful funerals, Ruth still trusted the Lord God of Israel and became spiritually a member of the nation God had chosen. Three graves seemed to testify that death was in control, but Ruth trusted God to guide and provide. Take time now to read Romans 5, and as you read, identify four "kings" that reign in this world: death (vv. 14, 17), sin (v. 21), grace (v. 21), and those who trust Jesus (v. 17). Jesus enables us to "reign in life" because we are members of the kingdom through faith in King Jesus, our Lord and Savior.

What does it mean to "reign in life"? It means to trust Christ to be in control, no matter what feelings are within us, circumstances are around us, or consequences are before us. It means to live victoriously "on top of the circumstances" and not be smothered "under the circumstances." It's Moses trusting God day by day as He led Israel through the wilderness. It's David doing God's will as King Saul pursued him and tried to kill him. It's Jesus going up to Jerusalem, knowing that there He would be rejected, humiliated, and crucified. To reign in life is Paul aboard a sinking ship in a terrible storm, encouraging his fellow passengers, and publicly thanking God (Acts 27). It means God is King of my life and your life and that we gladly "trust and obey," walking in faith and not by sight.

You can see the Lord's hand and heart in every event recorded in the book of Ruth. Naomi and her husband and two sons were wrong to leave Bethlehem ("house of bread") and go to Moab, but when we don't allow God to rule, He over-rules. The three men die, leaving three widows behind. One returns to her pagan home, the second journeys with her mother-in-law to Bethlehem. The wealthiest unmarried man in Bethlehem comes to his fields just as Ruth is there gleaning after the harvesters—I think it was love at first sight, but I can't prove it! Ruth submitted herself to her mother-in-law and ended up at the feet of Boaz, her kinsman redeemer. He took every step necessary to take her as his wife, they wed, the entire community rejoiced, and God gave them a special descendant—David, the beloved king of Israel!

Judges is the book of "no king," but Ruth is the book of "the Lord is King"; and because He *is* King, we can "reign in life through One. Christ Jesus." All of this can take place *now,* in spite of what is going on in the rest of the world around us. And because we reign in Christ and serve in Christ, we can make a difference in this world.

ADVENTURE ASSIGNMENT #5

How is it possible for the beautiful experiences described in the book of Ruth to take place during a period in history when selfishness reigned and God was ignored? How do we locate the good and wholesome events when bad news saturates the media? It's easy to enjoy the happy events, but how do we endure the sad events? Find some Bible verses that deal with this problem.

Chapter 6

Man's King and God's King

First and Second Samuel

Samuel was the godly son of godly parents and the Lord used him to discipline Israel's first king, Saul, and anoint their greatest king, David. When God permits us to get our own way, we can be sure that trouble lies ahead. When there is gross sin among spiritual leaders, we can be sure there will be disgrace and defeat.

First Samuel: Man's King

Samuel, Kings, and Chronicles cover so much history, as well as so many personalities, that it would go beyond the purpose of this book to get lost in their extensive details. I strongly recommend you secure a copy of *A Harmony of Samuel, Kings, and Chronicles* by William Day Crockett (Baker Books). It will enable you to put the picture together and better understand the lessons God wants us to learn through these books.

In summary, though, Israel's elders begged the prophet Samuel to give them a king (1 Sam. 8). Sad to say, Samuel's sons were not godly men who could succeed their father in ministry. Samuel prayed to the Lord about the elders' request, and the Lord told him to give the elders what they requested, "for they have not rejected you, but they have rejected Me, that I should not reign over them" (8:7). This is the first of three "rejections" in Israel's history, when they rejected God the Father. The second occurred when Pilate offered to set Jesus free, the Jewish crowd rejected God the Son (John 19:15); and the third happened when the crowd resisted the witness of Stephen and stoned him, rejecting God the Holy Spirit (Acts 7:51). Once they had rejected the witness of the Holy Spirit, God could do no more to cure them of their blind unbelief (Matt. 12:31–32; Mark 3:28–29).

Fear of the enemy as well as lack of faith in the Lord motivated the Jewish elders to ask for a king. Their logic was this: the Gentile armies have kings and always win; we don't have a king; therefore, we will not win. Their logic should have run along these lines: our nation belongs to the Lord God; He is all-powerful; therefore, we trust Him to protect us and give us victory. The Lord selected Saul, the son of Kish, and Samuel anointed him king. He was tall, apparently muscular and good-looking, and the people admired him and accepted him.

The early days of Saul's reign were encouraging, but then things began to change. Saul failed to wait for Samuel the prophet; instead, he went ahead and offered the sacrifices (1 Sam. 13).

When Samuel confronted him for serving like a priest, he gave a lame excuse and blamed the people. Leaders who are impatient and good at making excuses are rarely good at anything else. Saul spared Agag, the king of the Amalekites, and Samuel rebuked him for his disobedience. It was then that Samuel broke fellowship with Saul and anointed young David to be the next king. From then on, Saul went from bad to worse. He opposed David (who had killed the giant Goliath) and tried to kill him. Then Saul, under cover of darkness, consulted with a witch to determine what he should do (1 Sam. 28; see also Lev. 20:6; 19:31; Deut. 18:9–13). Finally, he went out to lead his army, was wounded, fell on his sword, and died, and his sons died with him.

In his book *Profiles in Courage*, John F. Kennedy wrote, "Every one of us is in a position of responsibility: and in the final analysis, the kind of government we get depends upon how we fulfill those responsibilities. We, the people, are the boss, and we will get the kind of political leadership, be it good or bad, that we demand and deserve."[1] A theologian would say there are times when we want the wrong things, and the Lord disciplines us by giving us what we want. Mature Christians have learned to be grateful for unanswered prayers.

Please keep in mind that David always respected Saul's office even though he disagreed with his attitude and actions and was grieved by Saul's lack of godly leadership. In 1 Samuel 24, he calls Saul "my master" (v. 6), "the Lord's anointed" (vv. 6, 10), "my lord" (vv. 8, 10), "the king" (vv. 8, 14), and "my father" (v. 11). David had married one of Saul's daughters. But Saul was not a man of stable character. In 1 Samuel, we find that Saul loved David first

(16:23), then was angry at him, suspicious of him, and intent on killing him (18:8–11). Saul became afraid of David (18:12, 15) and finally openly declared his desire to kill his son-in-law (19:1). His son Jonathan's friendship with David led Saul to speak angry words of condemnation (20:30). Saul had lost the power of the Holy Spirit and opened his life to the powers of darkness (1 Sam. 16:14). "Man looks at the outward appearance, but the LORD looks at the heart" (1 Sam. 16:7).

Second Samuel: God's King

It has been said that everything rises or falls with leadership, and this is true. Saul left his nation defeated and confused, and God gave His people David to encourage and unify them. David already had proven himself a competent leader as well as a courageous soldier. David was born into the right tribe—Judah (Gen. 49:10)—and in the right town—Bethlehem (Mic. 5:2)—the eighth son of Jesse, a descendant of Ruth and Boaz (Ruth 4:18–22). People didn't pay much attention to David until after he killed Goliath and caught King Saul's attention. David was a faithful shepherd who cared for his father's sheep and even risked his life to protect them (1 Sam. 17:33–37). When Samuel went to Bethlehem to anoint David as king, he made the same mistake the nation had made when they judged Saul by his appearance. Samuel beheld David's seven virile brothers and expected God to choose one of them, but God rejected them all and chose David, "a man after His own heart" (13:14). For "man looks at the outward appearance, but the Lord looks at the heart" (16:7).

David had ministered to Saul with his harp whenever the king experienced one of his dark days (16:14–23). Of course, Saul's problem was much deeper—Satanic influence—but David's playing did soothe the troubled king. David was not only an obedient son and a courageous shepherd; he was also a brave soldier; a humble servant; and a gifted harpist, singer, and composer of sacred songs. Of the 150 psalms, half are attributed to David. It's unfortunate that, when some people hear the name "King David," they think only of his adultery with Bathsheba. Let's remember that he confessed his sins and suffered deeply because of them. The Lord forgave him and he paid the price for that forgiveness, and we should also forgive. Whoever is without sin among us may throw the first stone at King David (John 8:7). Because of David's sin with Bathsheba, four people died—the baby, Bathsheba's husband, and David's sons Amnon and Absalom. But when David took a census of the nation, seventy thousand people died (2 Sam. 24)! We tend to magnify sins of lust, but what about sins of pride leading to deliberate disobedience? We ask the Lord to cleanse us of our sins, and He does (1 John 1:9); but Paul commands us to "cleanse ourselves from all filthiness of the flesh and spirit, perfecting holiness in the fear of God" (2 Cor. 7:1). May we put away permanently those things in our lives that rob us of the blessings of the Lord.

On the battlefield, David was a hero, but with his family, he was far from a success. We have the names of eight wives—there must have been concubines as well—and fourteen children, but undoubtedly there were more. Amnon raped his half-sister Tamar and was murdered by her brother Absalom. Absalom formed an army and tried to capture the crown but was killed. Was court life tempting?

Did the children have too much freedom? Was David a better soldier and singer than father? Were his wives and children too much for him? Was he gone from home too much? Some of his psalms indicate that he had his share of burdens and cried out to the Lord for help. But David was God's king, and he looked to the Lord for guidance and strength.

ADVENTURE ASSIGNMENT #6

Read 2 Samuel 9 and meditate on it. What does this event say about David? What does it say to us about our heavenly Father?

Chapter 7

Solomon and Other Kings

Kings and Chronicles

David's many victories on the battlefield brought wealth into the treasury, and Solomon, his successor, used this to build the house of the Lord (1 Chron. 22; Ps. 132). David's great desire in life was to build the temple, but that was not God's will, so David provided the wealth and the plans so that Solomon was able to do the work. None of us can fulfill our personal dreams and desires all the time, but at least we can assist others to do the job.

There was peace during Solomon's reign, primarily because he married the daughters of the kings and queens of other nations and set up peace agreements. He had seven hundred wives and three hundred concubines, and they turned his heart away from the Lord (1 Kings 11:3). Solomon's wisdom impressed visitors who came from afar to hear him, but his worship of false gods grieved the Lord. The wisdom taught in the book of Proverbs is appreciated today, and so are the insights in Ecclesiastes and Song of Solomon. In Proverbs, Solomon is a teacher; in Ecclesiastes, an investigator; and in Song of Solomon, a lover. Proverbs is a practical book pointing the way to success. Ecclesiastes is a book about the problems and puzzles of life, and Song of Solomon is a deeply emotional book that urges us to grow in our love for Jesus Christ.

Solomon built the temple from the resources his father David supplied, and he brought prosperity to the nation. His speech and prayer at the temple dedication are both instructive, and the Lord's response that He heard Solomon's prayer and chose the temple as a house of sacrifice is most encouraging (2 Chron. 6—7). It's hard to believe that the man who said all these words and received God's great blessings should end up worshipping pagan idols!

Solomon also taxed the people heavily, and they asked for relief when his son Rehoboam succeeded him (1 Kings 12). Rehoboam's stupid decisions make it clear that we cannot inherit wisdom, and his arrogance and ignorance divided the nation. Does this mean that all young people are stupid and all adults are wise? Of course not! It means that we must get our counsel from the Lord and His people, young or old. Had the new young king listened to the experienced counselors, the nation's unity would not have been destroyed. Solomon was a wise man because he humbly asked for wisdom (1 Kings 3:1–16), and you and I can do the same thing (James 1:5).

The young should learn from the old and the old from the young—and both should learn from the Lord. Yes, there are old fools as well as young fools, but, generally speaking, an experienced adult who knows the Scriptures has more practical wisdom than an inexperienced teenager who has dropped out of church. Thanks to Rehoboam's lack of leadership, the nation divided into two kingdoms—the northern kingdom, comprised of the ten tribes of Israel, and the southern kingdom of Judah, comprised of Judah and Benjamin. Assyria conquered the northern kingdom and Babylon overthrew the southern kingdom.

Page through 1 and 2 Kings and 1 and 2 Chronicles, and you will meet a number of kings who failed and a few who succeeded. It was the same old story: obey the Lord, and He will bless you and protect you from your enemies, but do things your own way and to please yourself, and you will have trouble. Some imitated Solomon when they married heathen wives and led the nation into ruin. A few put the Lord first and removed the idols, and the Lord was with them to provide and protect. God sent Elijah and Elisha and other prophets to warn His people and call them back to godly living, and the people occasionally obeyed; but before long they drifted away again. A godly king would rescue the nation only to be followed by an ungodly king who led them back into sin. Remember that the prophets did not simply foretell the future but also told forth the truth of God to bring His people to repentance (2 Chron. 7:14). We could use that kind of ministry today. Because of those prophets, godly kings like Hezekiah, Josiah, and Uzziah reigned, honored the Word of God, and obeyed His will.

As far as I know, the nation of Israel and the born-again church of Jesus Christ are the only people on earth with whom the Lord has a covenant relationship, but Christian citizens of any nation may claim God's promises. The phrase "If My people who are called by My name" (2 Chron. 7:14) would surely apply to the church today (2 Cor. 1:20). We are commanded to pray for those in authority

(1 Tim. 2:1–7) and show respect to their office even if we disagree with them (Rom. 13:1–7). We must encourage civic righteousness—but only by our votes and our own obedience to the law. "Righteousness exalts a nation, but sin is a reproach to any people" (Prov. 14:34). We may criticize the sins of the unsaved, but it's the sins of the *believers* that hold back revival and the blessings of the Lord!

ADVENTURE ASSIGNMENT #7

Did the splendor of Solomon's kingdom bring glory to Solomon or to God or to both? If Solomon's many pagan wives influenced him to worship idols, how did his example influence the people in his kingdom? Why did Solomon move in that direction?

Chapter 8

The Triumphant Trio

Ezra, Nehemiah, and Esther

These three books mark the end of the Old Testament's historical section. As I already mentioned, Assyria had assimilated the northern kingdom, and Babylon had captured the southern kingdom. The prophet Jeremiah had predicted seventy years of captivity for the Jews (Jer. 25), and, with that time completed, it was time for them to return to their land. It was essential that the people be in their own land so they might maintain a separated life that glorified the Lord rather than adopt the ways of their pagan masters. God used Ezra, Nehemiah, and Esther to give the Jews a new beginning and to protect them from their enemies.

The People Return: Ezra, a Godly Priest and Scholar

The Persians had taken Babylon, and the Lord God of heaven moved Cyrus, their king, to allow the Jews to return to their land. "The king's heart is in the hand of the LORD, like the rivers of water; He turns it wherever He wishes" (Prov. 21:1). Ezra, a godly priest and scribe who had a profound and practical knowledge of the Word of the Lord, would become their leader. The Jews had been exiled because they had disobeyed God's law, and the only way they could be restored was to honor that law and obey it. The king also returned to the Jews the valuable temple furnishings so they could renew their worship of the Lord when their temple was restored. The whole enterprise was a gift from the Lord, a promise fulfilled, and an answer to their prayers.

The Scottish preacher Alexander Whyte said, "The victorious Christian life is a series of new beginnings," and this is true.[1] No matter how often we may fall, the Lord will lift us up and give us a new start. "The steps of a good man are ordered by the LORD, and He delights in his way. Though he fall, he shall not be utterly cast down; for the LORD upholds him with His hand" (Ps. 37:23–24).

As you read Ezra 3, note the unity of God's people, a good example for us to follow today. They gathered together (v. 1), stood together (v. 9), and sang together (v. 11). Then they built together (4:3). They knew that God's eye was upon them (5:5), and they trusted Him to help them deal with their enemies. Blessed are those believers who trust the Lord, obey Him, and work together to accomplish His will. Blessed are those children of God who know that God can meet their needs.

Ezra was not only a man of the Word of God, but he was also a man of prayer (Ezra 9), for the two go together (Acts 6:4). He prayed for God's provision and protection, and the Lord answered. Their journey's route was neither easy nor safe, but the Lord met every need. It took faith for them to refuse the protection of Persian soldiers (Ezra 8:21–23), but what a testimony of God's greatness! God's eyes were upon them, and His hands were guiding and protecting them.

How sad Ezra must have been when he learned that some of the people were compromising again and taking wives from among their pagan neighbors (ch. 9). Compromise with the world has always robbed God's people of a clear testimony and God's blessing (2 Cor. 6:11–7:1).

Ezra was an exemplary servant of God. He knew the Word of God and the God of the Word. He sought the Lord's blessing and had no fear of the enemy. He knew how to pray and encouraged others to pray. The Word of God was within him, and the hand of God was upon him (Ezra 7:6, 9, 14, 28; 8:18, 22, 31). He realized that it was the Lord's grace alone that enabled the remnant to return to their inheritance and worship and serve the Lord. According to Ezra, the remnant that returned to the Holy Land was like a nail or tent peg that God hammered in a safe place, a light in a dark place, and a wall of protection. The people were experiencing God's mercy and a revival like life out of death. As we serve God, we must look at our situation from His point of view and not our own.

The People Rebuild: Nehemiah, a Faithful Leader

"For who will have pity on you, O Jerusalem?" asked the prophet Jeremiah. "Or who will bemoan you? Or who will turn aside to ask how you are doing?" (Jer. 15:5). One man who stepped aside and asked about Jerusalem was Nehemiah, whose brother Hanani had just returned from a visit to the holy city (Neh. 1). The report Nehemiah's brother gave him was not encouraging. It broke his heart, and he "sat down and wept, and mourned for many days" while fasting and praying (Neh. 1:1–4). Similarly, the apostle Paul was in "great sorrow and continual grief" because of his people's blindness (Rom. 9:2). But when was the last time you heard a tearful prayer—or prayed a tearful prayer—for the salvation of God's chosen people?

Ezra was a priest and a scholar, and Esther was a queen, but Nehemiah was a humble Jewish layman who served the king wine at his meals. His grief over the ruins of the holy city moved him to weep and pray and give himself to the Lord to do something about Jerusalem. But he could do nothing without the king's approval. The king noticed that Nehemiah was not his usual self and that he was very sad. He asked him what was wrong. Nehemiah's brief reply led to the king asking him what he planned to do, and Nehemiah lifted up one of his "telegraph prayers" to the Lord. Nehemiah was a man of prayer, and in his book, you'll find ten such prayers (vv. 1:4–11; 2:4; 4:4; 5:19; 6:9, 14; 13:14, 22, 29, 31).

Privately, Nehemiah examined the situation and calculated what needed to be done. Preparation for labor is as important as the labor itself. Then he met with the city elders and challenged them to repair the gates and rebuild the city, and they accepted his challenge. Nehemiah used the pronoun "we" and not "you" because he intended to work beside them. Bosses use "you," but leaders use "we."

But there were also the "they" people, the enemies of the Jews around them who did not want the city restored (4:1–6). The enemy planned a sudden attack, but Nehemiah posted guards, and the people prayed for the Lord to protect them. This is the background for the phrase "watch and pray," which our Lord often used. If we watch and pray, we can overcome the world (Mark 13:33), the flesh (14:38), and the devil (Eph. 6:10–18). Successful workers are balanced; they keep their eyes open and their hands ready to work or to fight. Charles Haddon Spurgeon followed their example and called his church magazine *The Sword and the Trowel*. If all we do is fight, we build nothing; but if we build and are prepared to fight, we protect our work. Blessed are the balanced!

Chapter 3 makes it clear that the Lord uses all kinds of people with a variety of abilities to accomplish His work: men and women, leaders and ordinary citizens, craftsmen and laborers, and even people from surrounding villages. Their devotion to the Lord and His leader united and encouraged them. Some worked on the wall only before their own house while others worked in more than one location. Their faith was in the Lord, and they trusted Him to provide for them and protect them. I have been involved in two local church building programs and know what it means to look to the Lord for His guidance day after day—especially when, like me, you can't even read a blueprint!

The enemy tried many subtle devices to hinder the work and stop it, but Nehemiah knew what they were doing and avoided their traps. They invited him to meet with them and "talk things over," but Nehemiah said, "I am doing a great work, so that I cannot come down" (Neh. 6:3). (Our Lord could have quoted that verse when He was on the cross and the people told Him to come down!) Nehemiah and his people served a great God (1:5; 4:14; 8:6; 9:32) and had no time for devious detours. When the work was completed, the dedication service gave the Lord all the glory. No matter what your service may be, it is great because it is for a great God.

Nehemiah not only faced trouble from the outside but also from the inside, from his own people who did not obey the Lord. Some of the Jews even opened their doors to the enemy! Nehemiah had to deal with Jewish men married to pagan wives and people co-operating with the enemy. I fear that we have similar problems in our churches today as professed believers compromise with the world, the flesh, and the devil.

There is a need today for leaders like Nehemiah and for followers who rejoice in the greatness of the Lord and the opportunity to rebuild what others tear down.

The People Rejoice: Esther, the Courageous Intercessor

The book of Esther magnifies the Lord through the life of a beautiful Jewish girl who risked her life to save her people. Along with Esther, three other key characters appear in the book: her uncle Mordecai, who had adopted her and raised her; Haman, the king's crafty "pet officer," who hated Jews in general and Mordecai in particular; and the king of the Persian Empire, who made some bad decisions. I suggest you read the book in one sitting, paying close attention to the Lord's providential working in the lives of these four people. God is not mentioned in this book, and yet His hand is at work and His will is being accomplished from beginning to end.

The book spotlights an ancient malady, anti-Semitism, first mentioned in Scripture in Genesis 12:1–3, where the Lord tells

Abraham, "I will bless those who bless you, and I will curse him who curses you." Why would anyone curse the Jews? Simply because they are Jews, God's chosen people, the nation selected by the Lord to give the world the Bible and Jesus Christ the Savior. No nation, ancient or modern, has suffered as have the Jews, and yet they have contributed immensely to world history. Historian Paul Johnson, in the epilogue of his book *A History of the Jews*, wrote, "Certainly the world without the Jews would have been a radically different place," and he listed some of the contributions the Jewish people have made to civilization: the sanctity of human life; equality before the law; the dignity of the human person; social responsibility; and love as the foundation of justice, to name a few.[2] The Christian believer would add the knowledge of the one true and living God; the Bible; and Jesus, the Savior of the world. It's obvious that Satan hates the Jewish nation and uses every tool available to accuse them, attack them, and destroy them. Besides Genesis 12:1–3, consider Deuteronomy 30:7, Jeremiah 30:10, and Acts 18:2.

Such anti-Semitism pervades the book of Esther. Esther's inner beauty—her strength, wisdom, and godly spirit—made her perfect to lead the defense against such attitudes. Yet her story opens with allusions to her outer beauty.

Occasionally in Scripture, beauty leads to trouble. In Egypt, Sarah's beauty got Abraham into trouble because he lied about her (Gen. 12:10–28), and Joseph's good looks put him into prison because his master's wife lied about him (ch. 39). Similarly Esther's beauty captured the king, and she was forced into a life she didn't ask for. However, the Lord put her on the throne, the perfect place to be when all the trouble started. When the king foolishly approved

Haman's plan to slaughter the Jews, Mordecai knew that, humanly speaking, Esther was the only person who could intercede and save the nation. He admonished Esther to get the message across to the king before it was too late. God brought her into the kingdom for this reason! "Yet who knows whether you have come to the kingdom for such a time as this?" asked Mordecai (Esther 4:14), and her courageous reply was, "If I perish, I perish!" (4:16). Her prayers, faith, and courage mark her as one of God's heroines. What began as a tragedy ended as a celebration—the joyful feast of Purim, which the Jews have celebrated for centuries and still celebrate today.

ADVENTURE ASSIGNMENT #8

Esther has been criticized by some because she was part of a "beauty contest" and married an unbelieving Gentile. Do you agree with their criticism? Where do you see God at work in this slice of Jewish history?

Chapter 9

Five Unique Books

Job to Song of Solomon

These five books are especially valuable because they cover many aspects of human life: Job, Psalms, Proverbs, Ecclesiastes, and Song of Solomon. Job and his friends tell us that living involves *discussing* and even *debating*, while the psalmists teach us that living involves *discovering*. The psalms are like rich mines filled with gold, silver, and precious stones. King Solomon's collection of proverbs presents us with wisdom that involves our *deciding*, and laying hold of the truth in his *Ecclesiastes* involves *discerning*. The beautiful story in the *Song of Solomon* offers preparation for and an invitation to *delighting* in the beauty and love of the Savior. What a rich spiritual meal they set before us! If we don't rejoice in this spiritual dinner, perhaps we have been nibbling at too many cheap substitutes between meals!

Chapter 14

The Prophets

Zephaniah to Malachi

We come to the end of the Old Testament! I trust the journey was exciting and enriching and that you will make it many times over as you mine the riches of the Scriptures. Please note the Messianic references throughout Zechariah.

Zephaniah

This brief book deals with God's judgments against the kingdom of Judah and the surrounding Gentile nations that had opposed the Jews. Like some of the previous prophets we have met, Zephaniah wrote about the impending "day of the Lord" (1:7, 8, 14). The Lord had been long-suffering toward His people and the Gentiles, but now the time had come for Him to act. You find the Lord saying "I will" at least twenty-five times in these three chapters, announcing what He planned to do, and He did what He said He would do! Zephaniah was the great-great grandson of King

Hezekiah, so he had royal blood in his veins, but his only concern was to minister to his people and please his sovereign Lord.

In 1:1—2:3, the prophet indicted the people of Judah for their sins, especially their idolatry, and pleaded with them to repent and return to the Lord. Both the rulers and the priests were guilty. Note the "I will" statements in this section. In 2:4–15, the Lord warned the Gentile nations that He would judge them for their sins. Humble repentance was their only hope for deliverance.

Jerusalem was the target in 3:1–7, for the princes, judges, priests, and false prophets were leading the people astray. But verses 8–20 recognized the faithful remnant that would be true to the Lord and would be delivered. They would gather together as a great choir and sing the Lord's praises (14–15). Note that God the Father would sing as a mother would sing to a troubled child (3:17). God the Son sang with His disciples in the upper room (Matt. 26:30), and God the Spirit sings through the hearts and voices of His faithful people when they assemble for worship (Eph. 5:18–21).

Chapter 2 verse 13 mentions Nineveh as a target for judgment. The city repented when Jonah ministered there, but this time the Lord would not relent. The city would be destroyed.

Haggai

In the year 786 BC, King Cyrus permitted the Jews in captivity in Babylon to return to Jerusalem to rebuilt the temple and establish their lives. About fifty thousand returned. The king appointed Zerubbabel governor, Joshua served as the high priest, and Haggai was the resident prophet. We have records of only four brief messages that Haggai received from the Lord and gave to the people. However, God used them to spur on the struggling remnant that worked and worshipped in the midst of danger and distress. We might name these four messages "Be Ashamed" (1:1–11, with the people's response in 1:12–15), "Be Strong" (2:1–9), "Be Godly" (2:10–19), and "Be Encouraged" (2:20–23). The remnant did rebuild the temple and establish its ministry, and as a result, the nation was preserved. They and their successors built the bridge between the Old Testament and the New and kept the nation going that would bring the Son of God into the world.

Be Ashamed (1:1–15).

Of course, the first thing the people needed as they returned to Jerusalem was housing, but their primary task was to clean up the wreckage and rebuild the temple. Once the temple was finished, Joshua and his priests and Levites (Ezra 6:16) could offer the daily sacrifices and lead them in celebrating the various ceremonies that Moses gave them in the books of the law. However, the people pointed out that their priorities were confused because they were putting their own interests ahead of God's work. Because of this, the Lord could not bless them as He wanted to. I have been privileged to minister to many different congregations in many different kinds of buildings—one of them was built in the 700s!—and I have noticed that the church buildings that were best cared for housed people who loved the Lord and practiced Matthew 6:33. Their priorities were right. Let's rejoice that the

Jewish remnant admitted their sin, repented, and started working on the new temple. This pleased the Lord, He began to turn their "curses" into blessings, and the work prospered.

Be Strong (2:1–9).

I can't imagine what the temple ruins looked like or what a burden it was for the men to remove the debris and make room for new construction. "Be strong" (v. 4) was God's command, and His commandments are always accompanied by His enablements if we step out by faith. He accompanied "be strong" with "fear not" because fear brings weakness. Instead of looking to the Lord, we are looking at ourselves and measuring our strength. The new temple lacked the size and splendor of Solomon's temple, and this grieved some of the old people—remember that the "good old days" are a combination of a bad memory and a good imagination. The original temple still would have been there had the leaders and people obeyed the prophets and repented of their sins, but it was too late. Furthermore, the Lord would accept their work and bless those who ministered there if their lives and services were motivated by godliness, which leads to our third commandment.

Be Godly (2:10–19).

A godly, obedient person can't share his or her godliness with another, but an unclean person can share uncleanness. Personal obedience and devotion to the Lord always leads to blessings from the Lord so long as our desire is to glorify Him. We must keep clean and flee that which is defiled while devoting ourselves to that which is holy.

Be Encouraged (2:20–23).

The Lord gave Haggai a special message for governor Zerubbabel, for leaders carry heavy burdens and are often misunderstood and criticized. The Gentile nations didn't want the Jews back in Jerusalem, but the Lord guided His people and protected them. Doing the will of God for the glory of God is the best protection God's people can have. How important it is that we pray for our leaders and encourage them by our work and our walk.

Zechariah

Thirty-one people in the Bible were named Zechariah, but the one we're focusing on was a prophet during the time the Jewish temple was rebuilt. Like Haggai, he ministered to the remnant of Jews who had returned to Jerusalem from Babylon. In 2:4, he is referred to as "a young man," which puts him in with Daniel and his friends (Dan. 1:4, 6, 10, 13, 15, 17), Jeremiah (Jer. 1:6), Solomon (1 Kings 3:7–9), and Timothy (1 Tim. 4:12). The Lord calls and uses young men and women who are surrendered to Him. In Zechariah's time, there were elderly people among those who had returned to Jerusalem, so perhaps the Lord called younger servants to keep things in balance. Remember, these people faced very difficult circumstances and needed encouragement from the Lord.

Chapters 1 through 6 record eight visions the Lord gave Zechariah to convey truths that would encourage the builders. We won't go into detail—you can take that up in your own Bible study—but will only summarize the major message in each vision.

The prophet sees visions (1:1—6:15). In 1:7–17, God's servants *see* that God's will is being done as they patrol the earth and its inhabitants. (Note that the prophet's question in 1:9–10 is answered in 1:12–17.) The Gentile nations will *acknowledge* the kingship of Jesus Christ and *go* to the Holy Land to worship Him. According to chapter 9, there will be *peace* (vv. 1–10), *deliverance* (v. 11), *hope* (v. 12), *victory* (v. 13), and *beauty* (vv. 16–17) for Israel.

Malachi

Malachi's name means "messenger of the Lord," and he ministered to the people and their leaders who had returned to Jerusalem after the Babylonian exile. If you want to read parallel passages, turn to Ezra 9—10 and Nehemiah 8—13. The people did rebuild the temple, and the priests did carry on a ministry, but all was not well. The Lord could not bless them as He wanted to because the priests were not spiritual and the people were not enthusiastic about their faith. A church member once criticized her pastor for preaching a series of sermons on the sins of the saints. "When Christians sin, it's different from when unsaved people sin," she argued, to which her pastor replied, "Yes—it's much worse!" Jerusalem's citizens (including the priests) were guilty of all sorts of sins, and the prophet Malachi sought to bring them back to the Lord who had so graciously freed them from captivity.

But let's not criticize the ancient Jewish people until we examine our own lives first. When we read these four chapters, at least six serious questions about our Christian life confront us.

Do I love the Lord (1:1–5)? The Lord had often declared His love to His people, and Malachi opened his book with this affirmation, *but the people questioned it!* You can hear them saying, "If God loves us, why are the crops so poor? Why is the weather so bad?" The prophet explained why: the priests and people were not living for the Lord. "If you keep My commandments," said Jesus, "you will abide in my love" (John 15:10). We don't love God just so He will bless us but because a loving heart knows how to use His blessings for His glory.

Do I give the Lord my best (1:6—2:9)? When we give God our best, we honor Him and bring glory to His name. God can turn curses into blessings, or He can curse our blessings (2:1–2; Neh. 13:2). Notice how often the prophet speaks of God's name (Mal. 1:6, 11, 14; 2:2, 5; 3:16; 4:2). His name should be magnified beyond the borders and across the whole world (1:5, 11, 14). The priests were not bringing the Lord the best sacrifices (vv. 7–8), and serving Him was a burdensome weariness and not a joy to them (v. 13). King David had the right attitude: he would not offer the Lord that which cost him nothing (2 Sam. 24:24).

Do I honor the Word of the Lord (2:10–16)? Israel is a covenant nation, for at Sinai, they agreed to serve the Lord and obey His Word (2:4–6, 8, 10, 14; Exod. 19—24). The church is also a covenant fellowship through the blood of Jesus Christ (Matt. 26:28). The priests in Malachi's day had broken their covenant with the Lord (Mal. 2:1–9), and so had the people (vv. 10–12); the marriage covenant had also been violated (vv. 10–17). It's frightening today to see churches ignoring God's clear directions and imitating the world instead.

Do I weary the Lord with my self-defense (2:17—3:5)? At least seven times in his book, Malachi quoted the arrogant arguments of the people as they debate with the Lord (1:2, 6–7; 3:7–8, 13). "In what way did we do what you said?" they asked the Lord when He accused them of sin. They retaliated but did not repent. Jesus and John the Baptist are referred to in 3:1–3 as well as in 4:1–3, and they both revealed the sins of the people who debated with them.

Do I rob the Lord (3:7–12)? Not only were the people bringing the Lord imperfect sacrifices, but they were also not giving Him the tithes and offerings needed to support the ministry at the temple. They robbed the Lord and at the same time robbed themselves! How could the Lord bless their disobedience? The contemporary Christian doesn't live under the old covenant law; but if those under the old covenant could give tithes, surely Christians under God's bountiful grace could at least start there! Remember, when we rob God of what He enables us to earn, we are only robbing ourselves.

Do I serve the Lord with gladness or disdain (3:13—4:6)? "'Your words have been harsh against Me,' says the Lord" (v. 13). We may not be guilty of complaining to the Lord, but we might be lax in thanking Him for all we receive from Him. Let's belong to that blessed remnant described in 16–18: those believers who fear the Lord, meet together, record His mercies, and become His jewels.

When Malachi put down his pen, that was the end of the prophets for four hundred years; and then John the Baptist appeared to introduce the Savior to the world (4:5–6; Matt. 11:10–14; 17:10–13).

ADVENTURE ASSIGNMENT #14

Select one book of the minor prophets and read it carefully. Make a list of the admonitions and promises that are especially needed in your life and in the life and ministry of your church family.

Chapter 15

The Good News

The Four Gospels

The word *gospel* means "good news" and refers to the good news of Jesus Christ, the Son of God and the Savior of the world. The four writers give us accurate and enriching accounts of the Master: what He said and what He did for us. As you study, you will find a "harmony of the gospels" to be very helpful. There is no greater message than what these four books contain.

The Gospel of Matthew

When the Holy Spirit took hold of Matthew the apostle, He led him to write a New Testament Pentateuch—the first seven chapters of his gospel. He built a bridge between the Old Testament and the New Testament to make it easier for his Jewish readers to transition from Malachi to Matthew: "The book of the genealogy of Jesus Christ," began Matthew verse 1. The word translated "genealogy" or "generation" is the Greek word *genesis*, which gives us, naturally enough, the

English word *genesis*. Matthew 1 is the Genesis chapter of his gospel record. It is a genealogy of our Lord, starting with Abraham, the founder of the Jewish nation, and ending with Jesus Christ. These people are "living links" between the fall of Adam and the birth of our Savior.

In my early days as a believer, I usually skipped over the genealogies when I read the Bible; but I soon learned to appreciate them. It was very important that each Israelite be able to prove his or her lineage. If they didn't, they could not share in the material and spiritual privileges of the Jewish people (Ezra 2:59–63). The Bible contains at least twenty-four principal genealogies, the last two being of Jesus Christ, the Son of God. His biological line through Mary is in Luke 3:23–34, and the legal line through Joseph, his foster father, is Matthew 1:1–17.

Chapter 2 is the Exodus chapter of Matthew: "Out of Egypt I called My Son" (v. 15). King Herod wanted to kill Jesus, so the Lord directed Joseph to take the child and His mother to Egypt, thus fulfilling the prophecy in Hosea 11:1. No doubt, the generous gifts that the magi had given to them covered their expenses (Matt. 2:11). Just as the nation of Israel went to Egypt for protection when Joseph was second ruler in the land, so the holy family found protection in Egypt until it was time to return to the land of Israel.

In Matthew 3, John the Baptist introduces the Leviticus chapter, for though he is remembered primarily as a prophet, he was born into a priestly home (Luke 1). He identified the Messiah to the nation of Israel and exhorted the people to believe in Him and follow Him (John 1:19–34). John's baptism superseded the ceremonial washings of the Jews and prepared the way for their faith in Jesus. John the Baptist did not fret when Jesus' disciples baptized more people than he did (John 4:1–2) for he had announced, "He must increase, but I must decrease" (John 3:22–26, and especially v. 30). The Jewish religious leaders were very jealous over their God-ordained religion and were suspicious of anybody who proclaimed any other message.

The Numbers chapter of Matthew is chapter 4, where we find Jesus in the wilderness facing temptation by Satan. While marching toward their Promised Land, the people of Israel were in a wilderness, being tested by the Lord. They had the opportunity to enter Canaan but did not believe the Lord would keep His promises and give them victory over the enemy. "Would it not be better for us to return to Egypt?" they said (Num. 14:3). They rebelled against Moses and Aaron, fell into the trap laid by Balak and Baalam, and rebelled against the Lord. "But they sinned ... against Him by rebelling against the Most High in the wilderness. And they tested God in their heart ..." (Ps. 78:17–18). God was testing them, seeking to build their faith, and they were complaining and rebelling. Satan tempted Jesus in the wilderness, but He defeated Satan by quoting and obeying verses from Deuteronomy. Satan tempts us to bring out the worst in us, but the Lord tests us to bring out the best in us.

Matthew 5 through 7, called the Sermon on the Mount, comprises the fifth part—the Deuteronomy section—of our Pentateuch, another version of God's righteous law. God's holiness never changes, nor is it compromised, but the expression of that holiness may be altered. All of the Ten Commandments are repeated in the New Testament to apply to the church except the Sabbath Day commandment. The first day of the week—resurrection day, not the seventh—was the day the New Testament worshippers used. Paul wrote to God's people, "So let no one judge you in food or in drink, or regarding a festival or a new moon or sabbaths" (Col. 2:16). The emphasis in the Sermon on the Mount is on personal righteousness from within that honors the Lord as opposed to artificial "religious self-righteousness" just to win the applause of other people (Matt. 5:17–20).

The Gospel of Mark

His full name was John Mark. His mother, Mary, was a leading Christian in Jerusalem, and she opened her home to the believers (Acts 12:12). Mark was a cousin of Barnabas (Col. 4:10) and started out with Barnabas and Paul on their first missionary journey. But when the team arrived at Perga, Mark left them and returned home to Jerusalem (Acts 13:1–13). When Paul and Barnabas set out on their second missionary journey, Barnabas wanted to give his cousin another opportunity, but Paul protested. Paul questioned, "What can he do for the work?" while Barnabas asked, "What can the work do for him?" Both are important. The team split, with Paul leaving with Silas and Barnabas going with Mark (15:36–41).

Years later, Paul mended his damaged relationship with Mark, and they worked together again (2 Tim. 4:11). It was the apostle Peter who redeemed Mark and put him back into ministry (1 Pet. 5:13). Both 1 Peter 5:13 and 2 Timothy 4:11 indicate that Peter and John Mark were in Rome at the same time. What young Timothy was to Paul, John Mark was to Peter, and Peter called him "my son" (1 Pet. 5:13). Both Peter and Mark had failed the Lord—Peter by denying Him three times and Mark by abandoning his assigned ministry—so it would have been easy for them to bond.

Peter, led by the Spirit, gave John Mark the material found in his gospel. Note that Mark uses the name "Jesus" eighty-six times and "Christ" only seven times. Matthew wrote about Jesus the King and had Jewish readers in mind while Luke, which we shall explore next, wrote for Greek readers about the perfect and compassionate Son of Man. The theme of Mark's gospel is "Jesus the Servant of the Lord." There is no genealogy, for who cares where a servant came from? Mark wrote for the Gentiles, and you find him explaining Aramaic words and Jewish practices (3:17; 5:41; 7:11, 34; 14:36; 15:22, 34). The words they repeated in this book show that Peter and Mark understood the Gentile mind: *immediately* appears forty-one times and *amazed* nine times. Mark emphasizes Christ the teacher (thirty-nine references) as well as Christ the Servant of God and God's people. Mark makes it clear that Jesus is the Son of God, but he also portrays Jesus in His humanity (3:5; 6:6, 31; 7:34; 8:12; 10:14; 11:12). He uses action, details, and descriptions, the kind of writing that would appeal to his Gentile readers.

Consider what it meant to John Mark to have Peter mentor him. (Paul was mentoring Timothy.) When I look back on my own life, I give thanks for the "veterans" who prayed for me and gave me counsel. I determined to follow their example if ever the opportunities came, and it has been a great joy seeing the young men and women I mentored serving the Lord today. There is a desperate need today for the experienced servants of the Lord to make themselves available to the men and women who are just beginning their ministries and need occasional enlightenment and encouragement—especially encouragement. As you read the four gospels, note how Jesus mentored the men He had chosen.

Mark's focus on Christ as the Servant provides a model for us. All of God's people today should be servants of the Lord and of others (Eph. 6:6). The apostle Paul saw himself as a servant and not a celebrity (Rom. 1:1; 1 Cor. 4:1; Phil. 1:1). When I was teaching seminary students, I made it clear that pastors were servants of God and of their people and not the "bosses" of their congregations. A quotation from Andrew Murray on my study desk reminds me of this: "There is nothing so divine and heavenly as being the servant of all."

If the apostle Peter were available today to speak to us about Jesus' life and ministry, we would consider ourselves privileged people. Well, we have that privilege when we read and study the gospel of Mark.

The Gospel of Luke

Look carefully at the world of nature around you and the people inhabiting it, and you will soon conclude that our great God believes in variety. Read your Bible carefully, and you will come to the same conclusion. Take the writers of the four gospels: Matthew was a tax collector, Mark was a young Jewish believer, John was a fisherman, and Luke was a medical doctor. Luke was also the only Gentile writer of Scripture. Notice that the word *they* in Acts 16:6 changes to *we* in 16:10. Why? Because the author of Acts (who also wrote the gospel of Luke) had joined the group. (Watch for *us* and *we* in Acts 16:10–18; 20:5—21:18; and Col. 4:14.) Finally, read Acts 27:1—28:16 and Philemon 24. Luke was Paul's beloved friend and traveling companion as well as his helper in the ministry. I'm tempted at this point to get into a discussion about "Paul the friend" and the many people he named in his letters, but that would take us unnecessarily far afield. All I will say is that he took time to make friends, pray for them, love them, and greet them in his letters. In Colossians 4:14, Paul called Luke the "beloved physician." He was undoubtedly speaking for the whole church.

Now let's move from Luke's history of the early church to his account of the life of Jesus Christ the Messiah and the Savior of the world. Most Bible students select Luke 19:10 as the key verse in the book: "For the Son of Man has come to seek and to save that which was lost." Matthew exalted the King, Mark the busy Servant, and John the Son of God, but Luke the physician wrote about the compassionate Son of Man who ministered to others and brought them eternal life. Luke tells us in the first four verses of his gospel that he carefully investigated the information available about the life, works, and words of Jesus and, led by the Holy Spirit, wrote his book.

The gospel of Luke tells us that words like *must* and *should* were often on our Lord's lips, for He was a servant of God who had come to seek and save the lost. I have found at least eighteen "compulsive statements," starting with the words of Jesus at twelve years of age— "Did you not know I must be about My Father's business?" (Luke 2:49). Open your concordance and trace *must* or *had to* in Luke (depending on the translation you use) and discover the compulsive motivation of the Servant of the Lord.

Luke was a physician, so we can expect him to record our Lord's healing of the sick and afflicted. See 4:18, 23; 5:17–26; 6:17–34; and

8:40–56. Read the three accounts of the healing of the woman with the issue of blood (Matt. 9:18–22; Mark 5:21–34; Luke 8:41–48) and see how the three writers differed in their description of the woman's experience with her doctors. Luke, especially, described our Lord's ministry to women, including widows.

He also emphasized prayer. Jesus prayed when He was baptized (3:21), and He prayed all night before He chose His disciples (6:12). He prayed alone (5:16; 9:18), but He prayed with the disciples as well (9:28–29; 22:40–44). Finally, He prayed while on the cross (23:46). Luke's gospel contains numerous mentions of prayer in a general sense, including 5:16; 6:12, 28; 9:28; 11:1–4; 18:1–14; 21:36; 22:40–46; and 23:34, 46.

Since the Lord Jesus came to seek and save the lost, salvation is an important theme (6:9; 7:50; 8:12, 36, 48, 50; 9:24; 13:23; 17:19; 18:26, 42). Note in the hymn by Zacharias that salvation is pictured as the opening of prison doors and the granting of freedom through redemption (1:68), the cancellation of a debt through the remission of sins (vv. 76–77), and the dawning of a new day (vv. 78–79).

Jesus came to earth to serve, and He obeyed His father perfectly. "I have glorified You on the earth," He said to His Father. "I have finished the work which You have given Me to do" (John 17:4). I hope all of us can say that to the Lord when we get to heaven, for we who have trusted Christ are also here to serve. Paul called himself "a bondservant of Jesus Christ" (Rom. 1:1), but all believers are to be His servants, using our spiritual gifts for the glory of God and the good of others. In this way we can emulate Jesus as the compassionate

Son of Man. What we all want to hear Him say is, "Well done, good and faithful servant" (Matt. 25:23).

The Gospel of John

Whenever unbelievers ask me, "Where should I start reading the Bible?" I usually suggest they begin with the gospel of John. This book's purpose is to prove to readers that Jesus is the Son of God and to declare that faith in Jesus will save them. Those who put their trust in Him are born again and become the children of God (20:30–31). The word *life* is used thirty-six times in John's gospel. There are many "overviews" of the gospel of John. Some students outline the book with an emphasis on our Lord's miracles or the "I AM" statements He made. My overview focuses on three crises of our Savior:

> 1. They would not walk with Him (John
> 1—6; see 6:66)
> 2. They would not believe in Him (John
> 7—12; see 12:37)
> 3. They would not endure Him (John
> 13—19; see chapter 20)
> Conclusion:
> The resurrection of Jesus (chapter 20)
> The restoration of Peter (chapter 21)

If you compare those three main points with John 14:6, you find an interesting parallel. Jesus is the way, but they would not walk with

Him. Jesus is the truth, but they would not believe in Him. Jesus is the life, but they crucified Him. Yet He arose from the dead!

Another characteristic of the gospel of John is attention to people's spiritual blindness. When Jesus spoke in figurative language, His listeners took Him literally. Here are several examples of such moments:

> The temple of His body (2:19–21)
>
> Spiritual rebirth (3:1–7)
>
> Water of life (4:10–15)
>
> Bread of life (4:31–33; 6:41–46)
>
> Flesh and blood (6:51–59; feeding on the
>
> Word of God, 66–69)
>
> Returning to heaven (7:32–36; 8:21–22)
>
> Spiritual freedom (8:30–36)
>
> Physical death (11:11–13)
>
> Death (11:11–13; see 1 Thess. 4:13–18)
>
> Resurrection (11:23–27)

In the first chapter of John's gospel you find several names for our Lord Jesus Christ: The Word (v. 1), the true Light (v. 7; see 8:12), the only begotten Son (v. 18), the Lamb of God (v. 29), the Son of God (vv. 34, 49), the Messiah (v. 41), the King of Israel (v. 49), and the Son of Man (v. 51). The emphasis in this gospel is that Jesus is the Son of God (20:30–31; 1:34, 49; 3:18; 5:25; 9:35; 10:36; 11:4; 19:7). Besides John (20:31), the witnesses in this gospel that Jesus is the Son of God are John the Baptist (1:34), Nathanael (1:49),

Peter (6:69), the healed blind man (9:35), Martha (11:27), Thomas (20:28), and Jesus Himself (5:25; 10:36).

John often mentioned what Jesus had in His hands: a whip (2:15), loaves of bread (6:11), mud (9:1–7), a towel (13:4), and wounds (20:24–29; see Ps. 22:16). The apostle John included in his gospel Jesus' words to His disciples in the upper room (chs. 13—16) and our Lord's prayer to the Father (ch. 17), all of which are saturated with spiritual truth. He also provided facts about Judas, the traitor (6:66–71; 12:1–8; 13:2, 26, 29–30; 14:22; 18:1–5).

He also emphasized people who believed on Jesus: Nathanael (1:50), the disciples (2:11), the Samaritan woman and her friends (4:39), the nobleman (4:50–53), the blind beggar (9:38), Martha (11:27), and Thomas (20:28). One reason John wrote his gospel was so lost sinners might believe in Jesus and be saved (20:31).

The final chapter of John's gospel, chapter 21, gives us four pictures of the Christian life. We are "fishers of men" (vv. 1–11), but our toil is in vain unless we obey the Master (vv. 1–8). We are shepherds caring for the sheep (vv. 15–19), we are disciples following the Lord (vv. 18–23), and we are witnesses declaring the way of salvation (vv. 24–25).

John tells us much about Mary, the sister of Martha and Lazarus. We are first introduced to her and Martha in Luke 10:38–42 where Mary gave Jesus her *attention* as she listened to the Word. In John 11:28–33 she gave Him her *affliction* as she shared her sorrow over her brother's death, and in John 12:1–8, she shared her *affection* as she anointed the feet of Jesus with the precious ointment and wiped it with her hair. Little did Mary know that the accounts of her ministry would be written down in the Scriptures and shared with countless people around the world!

ADVENTURE ASSIGNMENT #15

Choose one of the gospels, read it carefully, and make a list of the individual people mentioned in it—the people who came to Jesus. Why did they come? Did Jesus minister to them all the same way? Did He help them all? Did any reject Him? Make a separate list of the people who opposed Him and how He responded.

Chapter 16

The Acts of the Apostles

Acts

Dr. Luke not only gave us one of the four gospels, but he also wrote a history of the early church. I suggest you pause and read the first chapter of the book of Acts, and as you read, note carefully what the believers were doing when they met in the upper room. Of course, the first thing they did was assemble, but that was just the beginning. The believers' actions in this chapter provide an index of many key activities of God's people, behaviors that would be seen throughout the book of Acts and throughout history—practices that ought to characterize every Christian and every church today.

Warning: don't look ahead. Make your own list before reading further in this chapter. Thanks!

They Assembled (1:12–14)

The apostles had received last-minute instructions from Jesus and then watched Him ascend to heaven. Two angels gave them further instructions, and the men returned to their "headquarters" in the upper room in the city. The words *together* and *one accord* are used twenty-five times in the book. Those believers not only belonged to the Lord but also to one another: "Now all who believed were together, and had all things in common" (2:44). The church was unified, and this included the mother of our Lord and other women who were believers (1:14). Jesus prayed that His people might be one, even as He and the Father are one (John 17:20–22). Spiritually speaking, true believers are one in Christ, but from a practical point of view, the church is terribly divided today and has a difficult time with unity. "And let us consider one another in order to stir up love and good works, not forsaking the assembling of ourselves together," wrote Paul (Heb. 10:24–25). If you want to know your responsibilities to other believers, take time to find the many "one another" statements in your New Testament.

They Prayed (1:14, 24)

There are thirty-three references to prayer in Acts, which is no surprise, for those early believers knew that Jesus spent hours in prayer and even prayed all night. He taught them to pray and was the perfect example of a prayer warrior. "And whatever you ask in My name," Jesus told them, "that I will do, that the Father may be glorified in the Son. If you ask anything in My name. I will do it" (John 14:13–14). Read Acts 2:44–47 and 4:23–31. When God's people stop praying, they start depending on their own abilities and ideas and begin imitating the world's methods. Many times over the years, in several different ministries, my wife and I have seen the Lord answer prayer for us and others, all to the glory of His name.

They Heard the Scriptures (1:15–26)

The Spirit of God moved Peter to quote Psalm 69:25 and 109:8, and this gave the believers the opportunity to replace Judas. The Lord wanted twelve apostles to minister to the members of the twelve tribes of Israel who would be attending Pentecost. Prayer and the Word of God always go together. The twelve apostles knew they were obligated to give themselves to the Word of God and prayer (Acts 6:4). The Old Testament priests also followed that pattern (Deut. 33:10), so did the prophets (1 Sam. 12:23; Dan. 9:1–3) and our Lord Jesus Christ (Mark 1:35–39). Believers need the Word of God so they know what to pray for and what God has promised to them (John 15:7). It has been said that all prayer and no Bible means heat but no light, while all Bible but no prayer means knowledge without action. God gives us the Scriptures so we know what to do, and He gives us prayer so we have the power to do it. Blessed are the balanced.

They Waited on the Lord (2:1)

The Holy Spirit was to come on the Day of Pentecost, so until that day dawned, the believers met daily for prayer and worship. To wait on the Lord doesn't mean to do nothing. Rather, it means to give God opportunity to prepare us for what He is preparing for us: "Whoever believes will not act hastily" (Isa. 28:16). "But those who wait on the Lord shall renew their strength" (Isa. 40:31). "Do not be like the horse or like the mule" (Ps. 32:9). (The horse is impetuous and wants to rush ahead, but the mule is stubborn and wants to lag behind or stand still.) The believer says to the Lord, "My times are in Your hand" (Ps. 31:15). Energetic people are prone to be impatient and challenge God's schedule, but this can only lead to confusion and defeat. The apostles wanted Jesus to set up the Jewish kingdom (Acts 1:6–8), but the Lord has better things in mind. There is a time when He will do that, but first the Holy Spirit had to come and baptize the believers and empower them for service.

They Received from the Lord (2:1–4)

They received direction from the Word of God and power from the Spirit of God. The Holy Spirit is mentioned fifty-seven times in Acts, and His ministry is seen in every chapter except chapter 3. I can never forget the words I once heard Dr. A. W. Tozer say: "If God were to take the Holy Spirit out of this world, much of what the church is doing would go right on; and nobody would know the difference." The Lord had promised His disciples that they would receive power (1:8), and He kept His promise. Believers today may claim that promise and receive the power they need to do the work God calls them to do. When you contrast Peter in the book of Acts with Peter in the Gospels, you see what a difference the Holy Spirit makes. If we wait upon the Lord, the power of prayer, the Holy Spirit and faith combine to bring victory in our warfare and blessing in our work. We can't be givers until we learn how to be receivers.

They Continued to Obey the Lord

What did they do? They "continu[ed] daily with one accord … [and] the Lord added to the church daily those who were being saved" (2:46–47). Today, most churches would rejoice if a few people were converted during the annual "revival," but the members of the early church led people to Christ every day! I like that phrase "continuing daily" (2:46) because it speaks of faith and faithfulness. Many people begin well but gradually drop out. We all need to "continue daily," whether at school or work or on vacation. *We are always witnessing!* However, who reaps the harvest is up to the Lord of the Harvest (John 4:34–38). "Moreover it is required in stewards that one be found faithful" (1 Cor. 4:2).

Yes, God's people should act "decently and in order" (14:40), but we should also be open to the freedom and variety that the Spirit occasionally wants us to experience. Dr. Bob Cook used to say to those of us who served with him in Youth for Christ, "If you can explain what's going on, the Lord didn't do it," and G. Campbell Morgan called the accounts in Acts "the regular irregularity of the Spirit's action."[1] In other words, people who are filled with the Spirit and led by the Spirit may seem eccentric to some, but in God's sight, they are continuing the work of the Lord, come what may. People thought Jesus was out of His mind (Mark 3:21–27) and that the apostle Paul was insane (Acts 26:24), and evangelist Dwight L.

Moody was called "Crazy Moody" in Chicago. The world doesn't understand Christians because Christians don't conform to the world (Rom. 12:1–2). May it always be so!

ADVENTURE ASSIGNMENT #16

Dr. A. W. Tozer said that if God took the Holy Spirit out of this world, most of what churches are doing would go right on, and nobody would know the difference. Do you agree with him? Based on your answer, how may we improve our ministries?

Chapter 17

Letters to the Believers

Romans to Colossians

The New Testament epistles are a gold mine of spiritual truth, written by people who were in the heat of the battle, winning souls and building and maturing churches. When you consider the many modern assets we have for transportation, communication, and education, you'll find that what Paul called "my deep concern for all the churches" (2 Cor. 11:28) cost much more in his day than it does today. Let's give thanks to the Lord for the wonderful tools we have and make good use of them, backed by Bible study, prayer, commitment, and patience.

The Epistle to the Romans

"I must also see Rome," said Paul (Acts 19:21), and anticipating that visit, he sent this letter ahead. He wanted the believers in Rome to know exactly what he believed and preached. As the capital city of the great Roman Empire, Rome was certainly a strategic place for the apostle to the Gentiles to minister, and he did finally arrive there—as a Roman prisoner. In this important letter, Paul pointed out what Rome needed and what the whole world needs today.

God's Truth, Not Man's Lies (1:1—3:20)

In the opening section of his letter, Paul first greeted the believers in Rome and complimented them on their solid faith and effective witness. He magnified Jesus Christ and the gospel. Then he put the Romans and other Gentiles on the witness stand and accused them of suppressing truth and believing lies (1:18–32). Their man-made pagan religion, with its many gods and goddesses, was certainly not true. The people could look around them at the natural world and know it had to be created and maintained by a great and glorious God. The pagan world not only suppressed the truth but also exchanged the truth for "the lie" (1:25; 2 Thess. 2:11). Note the emphasis Paul made on truth (1:18, 25; 2:2, 8, 20; 15:8). Paul used the word *righteousness* sixty-five times in Romans. There are multitudes of religious systems and philosophies in our world, but the only true worship of God is taught by the Spirit from the Holy Scriptures: "Indeed, let God be true but every man a liar" (Rom. 3:4).

Paul also declared the Jews guilty of lacking the saving righteousness of God (2:1—3:8). Their Old Testament Scriptures came from God and pointed the way to Christ, and the New Testament Scriptures clearly reveal to us Jesus Christ and the salvation found only in Him. Merely keeping the Law of Moses could never save

either the Jewish sinner or the Gentile. Both Jesus and the apostles
had to explain to the Jews that keeping the law could never cleanse
them of sin, and they needed to put their faith in Jesus Christ
who died for their sins. In 3:9–20, Paul wrapped up his case and
declared that the whole world is guilty before God and needs a
Savior, and that Savior is Jesus Christ, the Son of God, who died
for the sins of the world. Apart from the cross, there is no other
way to have our sins forgiven and be guaranteed a home in heaven.

Faith in Jesus Christ, Not Human Self-Effort (3:21—4:25)

Ask the average churchgoer how to get to heaven, and the reply
might be, "Keep the Ten Commandments." But Paul makes it clear
that the law cannot cleanse us from sin. The law reveals sin like a
mirror reveals a dirty face (Rom. 7:7; James 1:22–24), *but you don't
wash your face in the mirror!* Romans 7 tells us what the law does.
The law not only reveals sin, it also arouses sin (7:8–9) and ultimately produces death (7:10–11). All of this shows how dangerous
sin really is!

One of the key words in Romans is *justification.* Justification is
the gracious act of God whereby He declares the believing sinner
righteous in Jesus Christ. Don't confuse justification with sanctification, which is the process by which God makes the believer
more and more like Christ. In Romans 4, Paul made it clear that
justification is by faith and not good works (vv. 1–8), by grace and
not law (vv. 9–17), and by Christ's resurrection power and not
human effort (vv. 18–25). We don't work our way into heaven, but
we do live a godly life because heaven has come to us in the person

of the Holy Spirit. The law brings out the worst in us, but grace brings out the best in us!

The verse that summarizes this is "but the just will live by his faith" (Hab. 2:4; Rom. 1:17). It is also quoted in Galatians 3:11 and Hebrews 10:38. And it bears repeating: we are justified by grace—and not because we deserve it (Rom. 3:24). Instead it is by faith and not by our good works (3:28), comes by the blood of Jesus Christ (5:9), and is unto eternal life now and forever (5:18). Salvation is a wonderful gift!

Transformation, Not Imitation (5:1—8:39)

This section of the Roman epistle describes the depth and delight of the Christian life empowered by the indwelling Holy Spirit. Note the four "kings" in chapter 5: death reigns (vv. 14, 17), sin reigns (v. 21), grace reigns (v. 21), and the believer "reigns in life" (v. 17). In Romans 8—a thrilling chapter—we meet the Spirit of life (v. 2), the Spirit of death (v. 13), the Spirit of adoption (v. 15), and the Spirit of intercession (vv. 26–27)—one great and glorious Holy Spirit who, day by day, transforms us to become more like the Master (Rom. 12:1–2).

The Spirit of life imparts the life of our Lord into our lives: "if by the Spirit you put to death the deeds of the body, you will live" (8:13). In Scripture, adoption (v. 15) is not entering the family—we are born again into God's family—but being given an adult standing in the family of God. Babies cannot talk, walk, work, inherit wealth, speak, or carry burdens, but adults can. The moment you were born into God's family through faith in Christ, you were given an adult standing and can talk to your Father, understand what He says to you in the Bible, do adult tasks, walk, battle—yes, all the adult privileges and responsibilities are yours! We have no excuses—"I've been saved only three months. I can't do that!" Yes, you can! We all can! We have been given an adult standing in the household of faith, and the Holy Spirit enlightens us and enables us day after day.

Salvation comes through substitution because Christ died in our stead, but transformation comes through identification: "I have been crucified with Christ" (Gal. 2:20). When He died, my old self died with Him; and when He arose, I arose with Him into new abundant life. The world lives by imitation, one copying the other (Rom. 12:2); but Christians live by transformation, becoming more and more like Jesus. We are not "self-made" but Spirit made! "Christ died for me" is salvation, but "I died with Christ" is sanctification and transformation. To be identified with Christ through the Holy Spirit is the secret of the transformed life.

Others, Not Just Ourselves (Rom. 9—16)

Once Paul completed explaining the transformed life, he immediately challenged his readers to get busy serving others. These chapters instruct us to pray for the salvation of God's chosen people, Israel (chs. 9—11). When was the last time you heard public prayer for the salvation of the Jews? Paul makes it clear that believers today are debtors to the Jews (15:27), and that we should pray for their salvation and help get the salvation message to them.

But that isn't the only "spiritual debt" we have, for Romans 1:14 tells us we are debtors to a lost world and must pay that debt by our loving witness to the lost. We also are indebted to the Holy Spirit who lives within us (Rom. 8:12–15) and to weaker believers who need encouragement (15:1–14). Good citizens are good witnesses.

First Corinthians

Paul founded the church at Corinth and ministered there about eighteen months. A populous and prosperous city, it was proud of who its people were and what they accomplished. The Corinthians were especially proud of their "wisdom." But the city was also known for its corruption (see Rom. 1:18–32), and it was not easy to live the Christian life in such a place. Paul received personal letters telling of the church problems caused by some of the members, and he wrote the two Corinthian letters to correct their errors and answer their questions. Corruption and confusion infected the church. This outline summarizes the problem and Paul's letter:

1. **Corruption in the Church** (1—6)

   A. Members were divided about leadership (1:10—4:21)

   B. One member had defiled the church (5) The members were disputing and suing one another (6:1–11)

   C. Some were defiling their bodies with immorality (6:12–20)

2. **Confusion in the church** (7—16)

   A. Concerning marriage (7)

   B. Concerning idols (8—10)

C. Concerning church practices (11)

D. Concerning spiritual gifts (12—14)

E. Concerning the resurrection of the body (15)

F. Concerning the love offering (16)

The letter emphasizes the local church—what it is, what it should do, and how it should do it. Paul gave us several images of the church: a family (3:1–5; 4:15), a field (3:6–9), a temple (3:9–17), a loaf of bread (5:6–7), a body (6:15; ch. 12), an army (9:7), and a team of runners (9:25). This makes for a helpful series of sermons or Bible class lessons.

In the first nine verses of chapter 1, Paul described the church that the Lord made. But from verses 10 to 18, he focused on the church the people were building—and what he described is not beautiful. The church's problems were provided by the members of the church family! The spiritual leaders of the congregation were not faithfully teaching the people and uniting them in Jesus Christ. The city had gotten into the church and changed it when the church was supposed to change the city!

The church was divided because they fixed their eyes on human leaders and not on the Lord. One family liked Paul, but their neighbors liked Apollos, and another group liked Peter. Each group sounded spiritual, but their attitudes divided; and after all, the Lord did appoint apostles and other leaders to guide in the building of the church (Heb. 13:7–8, 13).

You will frequently find the words *wise* and *wisdom* in 1 Corinthians, referring to the wisdom we receive from God by the

Holy Spirit teaching us from the Scriptures. The "wisdom of this world" is not what feeds and directs God's people and God's work; it's the wisdom that comes from God. I fear many congregations today are imitating the world and ignoring the Word of God.

Acts 1:15–26 tells us that the first church was united, consulted the Scriptures, and prayed before they selected their leaders. In contrast, the city of Corinth was proud of their philosophers and their "wisdom," and Paul admonished them to get their wisdom from the Lord and not from the world. To attempt to build a spiritual church with only human ideas is to fail miserably, no matter how many people we attract.

In 1 Corinthians 3:9–17, Paul compared the church's ministry to constructing a building. Jesus Christ is the foundation (vv. 6–11), and we must build with God's wisdom in the Scriptures—"gold, silver, precious stones" (vv. 11–12), that which is permanent, not temporary. Ponder Proverbs 3:13–15 and 8:10–11. Throughout Paul's two letters to the Corinthian church, you will find him issuing apostolic orders to the church, and he expected the leaders to obey the Word of God. Church discipline is not easy, but at times, it is essential. Read 1 Corinthians chapter 5, which is a basic text on church discipline. It is exercised for the sake of the offender (vv. 1–5), the church (vv. 6–8), and those outside the church (5:9—6:8). The unsaved world watches the church, and when we permit sin to bring scandal to the church, we are destroying our witness to the lost world. The church knew about the man's sins and was even proud of their tolerance! Just as the Jews removed the leaven during Passover season, so the church must bring the sinner to repentance or remove the sinner from the fellowship. Church discipline is not "religious punishment" but loving family discipline.

First Corinthians 13 is perhaps the most familiar chapter in the book. It is often read at weddings and even funerals, but Paul intended it to be read at church services and business meetings to remind the saints that love is the essential element if a church is to enjoy purity and unity. We are to "[speak] the truth in love" (Eph. 4:15), for love without truth is hypocrisy and truth without love is brutality; God's people must avoid both errors. First Corinthians chapter 15 is perhaps the leading chapter on the doctrine of resurrection; the Sadducees did not believe in the resurrection—nor do some "religions" today—but Paul defended it admirably. I have often read parts of this chapter at the funerals of believers. It brings comfort to the hearts of God's people.

Second Corinthians

Paul knew that his letter had wounded some of his Corinthian friends, so he wrote another letter, our 2 Corinthians. It opens with *grace* (1:2), closes with *grace* (13:14), and scatters grace in between. Paul repeats the words *comfort* and *encourage*, but the word *suffering* is there also (1:3–11; 4:8–11; 6:4, 8–10; 7:5; 11:23–28; 12:7–10). However, Paul usually connected *suffering* with *glory*, so you will find that great word twenty-one times. His purpose in writing was to encourage his friends (and us) to stand firm in every difficult circumstance of the Christian life, trusting the Lord and seeking to glorify Him. Paul certainly experienced his share of suffering, but he learned to depend on God's grace

(12:1–13). He taught us in this letter that we can overcome discouragement by trusting the Lord for the grace of serving (chs. 1—7), the grace of giving (chs. 8—9), and the grace of obeying God's will (chs. 10—13).

The first seven chapters focus on the grace of serving. "If I have suffered," Paul wrote, "it's so God could comfort me and teach me how to comfort others!" Our Lord Jesus Christ had to suffer so that He might be a "merciful and faithful High Priest" and minister to us when we suffer (Heb. 2:17–18). Not all pain is punishment. Some of it is preparation for ministry. In 2 Corinthians 2:13–16, Paul mentioned "the Roman triumph," a very special parade to honor military heroes. When a Roman commander-in-chief and his army won a complete victory on foreign soil, killing at least five thousand enemy soldiers and gaining new territory for Rome, he and his men were honored by this parade when they returned home. For the Roman army, it meant honor and a victorious life, but for the prisoners, it meant facing the lions in the Coliseum. We may not have that kind of parade in this life, but just wait until we get to glory! Our Lord Jesus has won the war, and we are on the side of victory! Hallelujah!

Chapter 3 refers us back to the glorious, shining face of Moses (Exod. 34:29–34). Jesus had a shining face on the mount of transformation (Matt. 17:2) and so did Stephen when he was martyred (Acts 6:15). You and I may also have shining faces! Carefully read 2 Corinthians 3—4. Unlike Moses, we don't need to veil our faces because our light must shine in this dark world!

In chapters 8 and 9, Paul discussed the love offering he was receiving from the Gentile churches to help the needy Jewish believers. He explained that giving is a grace, which means we give in spite of circumstances, resources, and consequences. We must not give grudgingly but willingly and enthusiastically, and it must come from the heart. We give by faith, even as the farmer sows seed by faith, trusting God to give the harvest. Every Christian must learn the grace of giving. The principles of giving are in chapter 8 and the promises we claim in chapter 9.

Paul closed his letter (chs 10—13) with some very personal words from which we can learn a great deal. He appealed to the Corinthians to understand his ministry as an apostle, and he warned them that his enemies were saying things against him that were not true. Any man or woman who seeks to serve God faithfully will have critics and enemies *from within the church*! As an apostle, Paul had God-given authority to deal with troublemakers and was not afraid of them. His greatest enemies were those who claimed to be apostles but were only counterfeits. Paul hesitated to promote himself and boast about his ministry, but he had no alternative. He warned the Corinthians that he was coming to them in love but dealing with them with God-given authority. Like any good parent who disciplines a child for the child's own good, Paul dealt with offenders in love, but he did so with honesty and authority.

In this closing section of the letter, for the first time, he revealed his experience of going to heaven and coming back. To protect him from pride, the Lord gave Paul a thorn in the flesh and would not remove it. I'm a reader of biography and autobiography, and it's remarkable how many of God's servants have lived and served with painful handicaps. Pride is a dangerous attitude; it will ruin a servant's ministry and bring disgrace to the church. Just as children have "growing pains" during their adolescent years, so God's faithful people have "growing pains" as they mature in their walk with the Lord. Authority must be balanced with love and humility, and Paul had all three. We should too.

By the way, take your Bible and check the word *always* in 2 Corinthians: 2:14; 4:10–11; 5:6; 6:10; and 9:8. Talk about encouragement!

Galatians

Paul founded the churches in Galatia and taught the new believers the basics of church life, but some false teachers came along and told the fledgling Christians that faith wasn't enough. Those instructors said that they also needed to obey the Mosaic law if they were to be genuinely saved (2:16; 3:2–3, 10–14; 4:10, 21; 5:2–4; 6:12–15). The key verse to this book is 5:1. Look it up. Here is a simple outline that shows how Paul refuted those false teachers:

> 1. Biographical: Paul experienced the gospel
> (1—2)
> 2. Doctrinal: Paul defended the gospel
> (3—4)
> 3. Practical: Paul explained how to live the
> gospel (5—6)

If anyone knew the meaning of the gospel, it was Saul of Tarsus who trusted Jesus Christ and became Paul the apostle (1:10–24). His Damascus Road experience (Acts 9) not only saved him but transformed him into an energetic evangelist to Jews and Gentiles alike. The leaders of the Jerusalem church affirmed that he was truly born again and called to proclaim the gospel (Gal. 1:18—2:10). When he confronted Peter, who was being inconsistent about the law and the gospel, Paul won the battle (2:11–21).

To Paul, simply to experience and declare the gospel wasn't enough; he also defended it. Notice his pointed questions in 3:1–9, appealing to the Galatian Christians' personal experience. Righteousness comes by faith and not by practicing the Mosaic law. In verse 11, we meet Habakkuk 2:4 once again: "But the just shall live by his faith." (We also met it in Rom. 1:17.) The false teachers were denying both experience and Scripture! Abraham, the father of the Jewish nation, was saved by faith centuries before the law was even given (Gal. 3:1–9; Gen. 15:6). Why, then, was the law given? The law is like a mirror that shows us how dirty we are—*but a mirror will never be able to clean your face* (James 1:21–27)! The law reveals God's holiness and our sinfulness, and we seek deliverance from bondage and condemnation—and the law leads us to Christ, the only Savior (Gal. 3:24).

Paul points out clearly what the law cannot do.

- The law cannot justify the guilty sinner (2:16; Romans 4:5)
- The law cannot give righteousness (2:21)
- The law cannot impart the Holy Spirit (3:2)
- The law cannot give us an inheritance (3:18)
- The law cannot give us life (3:21)
- The law cannot give us freedom (4:8–10)

What the law can't give us, Jesus Christ can, and He does it when we trust Him. When the rich young ruler tried to keep the law, it brought him to Christ (Matt. 19:16–22), but he refused to trust Him.

What are the evidences that sinners who have trusted Christ have salvation? For one thing, they receive a new life that brings freedom (Gal. 5:1–15) and helps to produce spiritual fruit (vv. 16–26). They have a new fellowship that enables them to bear others' burdens and to share their burdens with others (6:1–5). Love motivates them, not the law (5:6, 13–14, 22). They discover that the law brings fear, but grace brings joyful freedom and growing love for the Lord and His people—and the lost!

The point Paul sought to make is that faith unites us with Jesus Christ and His life, love, and power; and these enable us to obey and glorify Him. The key verse says it well: "Stand fast therefore in the liberty by which Christ has made us free, and do not be entangled again with a yoke of bondage" (5:1). If you take the yoke of the law, you become a prisoner (5:1; Acts 15) and a debtor (Gal. 5:2–6)!

The old nature knows no law—there is no law strong enough to change or control us—but the new nature *needs no law*! The Holy Spirit enables us to know God's will and to obey it joyfully. I once heard about some prisoners who worked hard to dig a tunnel to escape from the prison. When they got to the end, they found themselves in the very courtroom where most of them had been tried and convicted! So it is with the believer who abandons freedom in Christ for bondage under the law.

Let's take our freedom seriously, guard it courageously, and use it lovingly.

Ephesians

Turning the page from Galatians to Ephesians is like leaving a battle-field and going high into the Alps, but both letters are inspired and important. The key theme in Ephesians is "in Christ," a phrase used 164 times in Paul's letters. Because the Holy Spirit dwells in us (2:22), we are "in Christ"; and because we are "in Christ," we have all we need to live for Christ and serve Him. All this and more is ours because of "the riches of His glory" (3:16). Here's a suggested outline:

1. Enriched in Christ (1)
2. Alive in Christ (2)
3. United in Christ (3)
4. Walking in Christ (4—6:9)
5. Victorious in Christ (6:10–24)

Enriched in Christ (Chapter 1)

In Christ, we have been blessed with the riches of His grace, which means "every spiritual blessing … in Christ" (1:3). Just as babies are born with all they need for sustaining life and growth, so God's children are "born again" with all they need to mature in Christ, live for Christ, and serve Christ. The word *grace* opens the book (1:2), closes the book (6:24), and shows up ten more times in between. It has well been said that God in His mercy doesn't give us what we do deserve but in His grace gives us what we don't deserve. Praise the Lord!

The letter opens chapter 1 (vv. 3–14) with a hymn of praise to the Trinity—the Father (vv. 3–6), the Son (vv. 7–12), and the Holy

Spirit (vv. 13–14). Our salvation involves the Father who chose us, the Son who died for us, and the Holy Spirit who sealed us and dispenses our spiritual inheritance to us. All believers, if they are walking with Christ in the Spirit, have the entire Godhead ministering to them! Through the Bible, the Spirit reveals to us how rich we are. Here are some items from our "spiritual bankbook":

- His goodness (Rom. 2:4)
- His glory (Rom. 9:23; Eph. 3:16)
- His wisdom (Rom. 11:33)
- His grace (Eph. 1:7; 2:7)
- His inheritance in the church (Eph. 1:18)
- Unsearchable riches (Eph. 1:18)
- Our understanding (Col. 2:2)
- Our needs (Phil. 4:19)
- Our enjoyment (1 Tim. 6:17)

There are two prayers in the letter. The first one (1:15–23) asks the Lord for *enlightenment*, "wisdom and revelation in the knowledge of Him" (v. 17); the second one (3:14–21) asks for *enablement*, the ability to know God's will and the power to do it. All this must be done in love.

Alive in Christ (Chapter 2)

Unsaved sinners are spiritually dead, but when they trust Christ, they are raised from the dead and given eternal life. "He who believes in the Son has everlasting life" (John 3:36). Besides the

resurrection of Jesus, the gospels record three other resurrec-
tions: a young man (Luke 7:11–17), a twelve-year-old girl (Luke
8:40–56), and the older man Lazarus (John 11). In each one,
evidence proved the person was now alive. The young man sat
up and spoke, the girl walked and had an appetite for food, and
Lazarus came to the door of the tomb where they removed the
not-so-fragrant grave clothes and dressed him with the garments
of the living. In Scripture, changing clothes symbolizes beginning
new life (Col. 3:1–17). When I became a Christian, I received a
new walk and appetite, my speech changed, and I "took off" some
things in my life that just didn't belong there.

United in Christ (Chapter 3)

The word *mystery* has nothing to do with puzzles or obscure thinking. In the Bible, a mystery is a secret truth, hidden by God and
revealed later. Jesus taught the mysteries of the kingdom (Matt. 13),
and Paul revealed the mystery of Jews and Gentiles united in one
body (Gal. 3:26–29; Col. 3:9–11). In Ephesians, Paul, alluding to
this mystery, used the word *together* in verses 1:10; 2:5–6, 21–22;
and 3:6. We are "all one in Christ Jesus" (Gal. 3:28). That's why
Paul used phrases like "the whole building" (Eph. 2:21), "the whole
family" (Eph. 3:15), and emphasized the oneness of the church.

Walking in Christ (4—6:9)

Despite what you may see on television, dead people do not walk.
Paul used the word *walk* to describe the Christian life because

every child of God should be standing upright and progressing in his or her spiritual life. This portion of Ephesians provides practical advice for walking as God intends and can be summarized as follows:

- Walk worthy of your calling (4:1–16)
- Don't walk like unbelievers (4:17–32)
- Walk in love (5:1–6)
- Walk as children of light (5:7–14)
- Walk carefully (5:15–17)
- Walk in harmony (5:18—6:9)
    ◊ Husbands and wives (5:21–33)
    ◊ Parents and children (6:1–4)
    ◊ Masters and servant (6:5–9)

Victorious in Christ (6:10–24)

That last "walk" deserves some comment: God's people are soldiers whom our enemy Satan and his demonic forces attack. It's important that we put on the armor of God by faith as we begin the day. Day or night, whenever we sense Satan at work, we can claim victory by faith. When King David laid aside his armor, the enemy defeated him disastrously (2 Sam. 1). The Word of God is our sword, and we must be able to recall the verses that meet our needs. Each morning, I put on the armor from head to foot—first the helmet of salvation, then the breastplate of righteousness, and so on to the shoes of peace. But the armor's effectiveness depends on our faith in God's promises. The helmet protects your mind, the breastplate your heart, the shield your body, and so on. Claim protection and victory by faith and the Lord will give you both.

Philippians

Acts 16 recounts the founding of the church at Philippi. Paul was a prisoner in Rome when he wrote this letter to thank the Philippian believers for the generous gifts they had sent him. The letter is a treasury of inspired truth, with insights on Christian joy and Christian ministry being uppermost. If I were back teaching seminary students preparing for ministry, I would discuss this book with them. It answers the important question, "What does Christian ministry involve?"

Ministry Involves Life and Death (Chapter 1)

Paul wrote, "For to me, to live is Christ, and to die is gain" (1:21). Ministry isn't a small part of life or even a big part of life; *it's all of life!* We give ourselves to the Lord unconditionally, follow Him faithfully, and obey Him joyfully. In our churches, we may see the pastoral staff, officers, and teachers as leaders, when, in reality, they are servants—the servants of God and God's people. They are following the example of Jesus, who said, "I am among you as the One who serves" (Luke 22:27). Paul wrote that he wanted Christ to be magnified in his ministry "whether by life or by death" (Phil. 1:20), and he certainly had his share of trials and dangers (2 Cor. 11:16—12:10). Paul had his friends in his heart (Phil. v. 7) and in his prayers (vv. 9–11), and he was willing to give his life for the spread of the gospel and the glory of God. The world doesn't pay much attention to it, but there are many prisoners and martyrs today for the cause of the gospel. We may not die because of our faith, but we must be willing.

Ministry Involves Sacrifice and Service (Chapter 2)

This chapter introduces us to four persons who knew what it meant to sacrifice and serve: our Lord Jesus Christ (vv. 1–11), the apostle Paul (vv. 12–18), Timothy (vv. 19–24), and Epaphroditus (vv. 25–30). We all need the "mind of Christ" when it comes to sacrifice and service. Jesus welcomed the children and blessed them. He helped the sick and afflicted. He shared the truth of God's Word and patiently taught His disciples. He willingly accepted the cross and suffered to save a lost world. His humility turned into honor and glory! Jesus must always be our example in everything we say and do. He was humble, and the Father honored Him with glory and rewarded His obedience with honor and power.

Paul suffered for his Lord (vv. 12–18) and could "work out" God's will because God was "working in" him. We are not manufacturers: we are distributors of what God shares with us. Paul went to the hard places, gave his best, and the Lord blessed Him. It's been my privilege over the years to mentor several young people who today are faithfully serving the Lord.

Some Bible students believe that Epaphroditus is the same man as Epaphras (a shortened version of the name) who helped found the church at Colosse (Col. 1:7; 4:12). Whether this is true or not, Paul thought highly of him and called him a brother, a fellow worker, and a fellow soldier, which is surely a compliment. While serving Paul in

Rome, he became ill and almost died. Epaphroditus knew something about sacrifice and service. What a great privilege it was for Timothy and Epaphroditus to labor with Paul.

This reminds me to encourage you again to investigate the many friends of Paul named in Acts and Paul's letters. Paul was not a "loner." He had many friends, taught them, encouraged them, and enlisted them in the work of the Lord.

As you read Paul's letter to the believers in Philippi, you no doubt noticed his emphasis on *joy*. Paul was a prisoner in Rome when he wrote this letter, yet he had "the joy of the Lord" in his heart and shared it with others. Child Evangelism Fellowship has a song that says, "Jesus and Others and You, what a wonderful way to spell joy!"[1] and Paul would agree with it.

Ministry Involves Gains and Losses (Chapter 3)

"But what things were gain to me, these I have counted loss for Christ" (3:7). When it comes to religion, Saul of Tarsus ranked at the head of the class. He was zealous for the Jewish faith and had authority to persecute and even imprison Jews who became Christians. His experience on the Damascus Road ended that, and the Jews started to persecute *him*! He lost favor with the Jewish religious leaders but experienced the favor of the Lord on his life and ministry. His self-righteousness disappeared, and the righteousness of the Lord took over. He lost some friends but gained many more, including Gentiles! He lost tradition and ritual and gained truth and reality. He had new goals in life: "that I may know Him and the power of His resurrection, and the fellowship of His sufferings, being conformed to His death" (3:10). Loss and gain!

That last verse (3:10) has always fascinated me. For example, three times Jesus took Peter, James, and John apart from the other disciples: at the mount of transfiguration (Matt. 17:1–13)—"that I may know Him"; when raising Jairus's daughter from the dead (Luke 8:41–54)—"and the power of His resurrection"; and while praying in the garden with Jesus (Mark 14:32–42)—"and the fellowship of His sufferings." Mary of Bethany is also linked to this verse. She sat at His feet to hear the Word (Luke 10:38–42)—"that I may know Him"; she saw her brother raised from the dead (John 11)—"the power of His resurrection"; and she anointed Jesus for His death and burial (John 12)—"the fellowship of His sufferings."

To stand still in the Christian life is only to go backward. Paul knew that he had not arrived at the ultimate stage in his spirituality, so he pressed on by the grace of God, and so should we (Phil. 3:12–16). We should grow in the knowledge of Christ, in the power of Christ, and in the suffering we experience for and with Christ (1:29). A stagnant Christian life is not a joyful or fruitful Christian life.

Ministry Involves Problems and Peace (Chapter 4)

I wish we knew why the two women Paul mentioned in chapter 4, Euodia and Syntyche, were not getting along, but Paul didn't give us the details. Whether we like it or not, debates, divisions, and disgraces punctuate church history. Christians are not perfect, nor are the outsiders who criticize them. It's been my privilege to pastor three churches, and in each of them, we dealt with a few troublemakers. Paul had a special affection for the believers in Philippi, and he implored the two ladies to forgive each other and get back in fellowship with the Lord and the church family. He also wrote about those "whose god is their belly … who set their minds on earthly things" (3:17–21). There is usually a group of carnal Christians in a church—saved but not separated. Like Paul, we weep over them and pray for them.

Paul ended his letter with warm and practical encouragement. The answer to all our needs and problems is faith in Jesus Christ. Are you worrying? Ponder verses 6 and 7. Does your task seem too difficult? Lay hold of verse 13. Is there a pressing need in your life? Verse 19 is the key to having what God wants you to have.

Colossians

Paul didn't found the church of Colosse but only heard the news that the Lord had blessed the work of Epaphras, possibly a member of the church at Ephesus. The saints in the Ephesian church were so faithful in their witness that "all who dwelt in Asia heard the word of the Lord Jesus, both Jews and Greeks" (Acts 19:10). But Paul also heard that problems developed in the church because false teachers had crept in and were causing trouble. In His parable of the tares (weeds), Jesus teaches us that wherever the Lord plants the good seed (God's people), the devil plants counterfeit Christians (weeds). If church leaders are not faithful to interview new members carefully, the devil's crowd will move in and take over. Paul couldn't go to Colosse and minister personally, so he sent them this letter which, to me, seems like the record of a series of questions Paul would ask the members of the church.

Are You a Christian? (1:1–14)

In verses 1–8, Paul described the characteristics of true believers. They have faith in Christ, they love God's people, and they look forward to Christ's return—faith, hope, and love. In other words, they have experienced God's grace, and this leads to a "walk worthy of the Lord" (v. 10). They grow in their knowledge of the Lord and live by the power of the Lord. They know they are saved only by the blood of Christ (v. 14). If you are a Christian, your sins have been forgiven!

Do You Really Know Jesus? (1:15–29)

He is the eternal Son of God, the Creator of all things, and the One who holds all things together. He is the Head of the church whose death and resurrection made the church possible. But especially notice what our attitude toward Christ should be: "that in all things He may have the preeminence" (v. 18). Please note that Paul wrote "all things" and not "some things." Because He is Master of all things, we are "complete in Him" and possess through Him all that we need for life, death, and eternity. In both Galatians and Ephesians, Paul declared that Christians are "one in Christ," and here in Colossians we are "complete in [Christ]" (2:10; 4:12). Jesus is beloved of the Father (1:13) and the Savior of the world (1:21–23).

But why is it so important that we grow in our knowledge of Jesus? Because the better we know Him, the more we will love Him;

and the more we love Him, *the more we will obey Him*! In 1:24–29, Paul tells us he suffered as he served the church, constrained by a love for Christ (2 Cor. 5:14). We study the Bible that we might know Jesus better and love Him more. After all, He is the Savior of the world, having united believing Jews and Gentiles in one body, the church.

Do You Recognize and Oppose the Enemies of the Church? (2:1–19)

People who mixed pagan philosophy with the Christian faith (vv. 1–10) as well as Jewish legalism (vv. 11–17), oriental mysticism (vv. 18–19), and asceticism (v. 23) had infected the Colossian church. God's truth needs no "seasoning," and attempts to please everybody only lead to disaster. Every believer should have "full assurance of understanding" based on the Word of the Lord (v. 2). To dilute the inspired Word of God is to grieve the Spirit of God, divide the church of God, and rob us of the blessings of God that He wants to send His people. God's "treasures of wisdom and knowledge" give all preeminence to Jesus Christ alone (v. 3). Paul warned that these false teachers try to deceive God's people (v. 4), cheat them (v. 8), judge them (v. 16), and defraud them (v. 18). Beware!

Do You Know What the Church's Doctrinal Treasures Are? (2:20–4:6)

Paul moved from the negative to the positive and exhorted the Colossians to relate everything to Jesus Christ and not meddle with the devil's lies. When we trusted Christ as Savior and Lord, we died

with Him and were raised in Him to new life. Our identification
with Jesus Christ is what makes it possible for us to draw upon
His spiritual riches and walk to please Him. Thus we become more
and more like our Lord (3:5–10)! It makes for a unified and godly
church when God's people realize how rich they are in Christ and,
by faith, draw upon these riches (3:11–17; Eph. 1:3). In 2:6–7,
Paul reminded us that we are responsible to walk in Christ, be
rooted in Christ, and be built up and established in Christ. This
means much more than an hour or two in church every week! Every
Christian is responsible to live like a Christian at home (3:18–21),
in the workplace (3:22—4:1), in the prayer closet (4:2–4), and in
the community (4:5–6).

What Spiritual Gift Can You Share with the Church Fellowship? (4:7–18)

A true church composed of real Christians is not a collection of
religious cliques but a family of people who love the Lord and one
another. Each person has at least one spiritual gift and should use
it for the building of the church body. Read this list in Ephesians
4, review the list in Romans 16, and discover the variety of people
who helped build the early church. Then read 1 Corinthians 12. If a
person unites with a local church but refuses to use the gift or gifts
the Lord gave them, that person is not walking with the Lord—or
perhaps not even born again!

ADVENTURE ASSIGNMENT #17

As evidenced by the books we've looked at in this chapter, people are different, and people are important. Review the "one another" statements throughout the New Testament. Discover how to get along with others and enjoy God's blessings.

Chapter 18

Letters to the Believers

First Thessalonians to Philemon

First Thessalonians

On his second missionary journey, Paul planted the church in Thessalonica, the capital city of Macedonia (Acts 17:1–9). In this letter, he sought to stir up their memories of his ministry and what he had taught them (1 Thess. 1:3; 2:9; 3:6). Memory is a gift from the Lord, and the way we use it makes it either a marvelous tool or a merciless weapon. Imagine what life would be like if we didn't have our memories. We would have to keep re-learning everything from our name and address to the multiplication tables to how to drive an automobile to how to read a book. When Paul wrote these two letters, he asked the believers to use their memories and recall his ministry among them. *Paul usually did things right and said things right the first time and didn't need to keep repeating and repairing things later.* The outline of the first letter is quite simple:

1. Life: remember the beginning of the church
(1—2)
2. Truth: remember the admonitions I gave
you (3:1—4:12)
3. Love: remember the encouragements I gave
you (4:13—5:28)

From the beginning, this church was an exemplary group of people that we would do well to emulate today (1:3–10). Faith, hope, and love are basic to an effective Christian life, and so is power from the Holy Spirit. These new believers turned from the world and imitated Paul and his associates, men who were worthy of their trust. God blesses churches that have godly leaders. The Thessalonian believers received the Word of God joyfully and shared the gospel with others in a wide area around them. They abandoned their idols and centered their new lives on Jesus Christ, who promised to come again. (We don't know when Jesus is coming for His people, so we live expectantly day after day.)

After complimenting the church on its exemplary conduct and ministry, Paul reminded them that, when he was with them, his own life and work were exemplary (ch. 2). We reproduce after our kind, and leaders must live the life they want their people to live (1 Tim. 4:12). Paul was a faithful steward of God's Word (1 Thess. 2:1–6) and treated the people as a loving mother cares for her children (2:7–8). "Love never fails" (1 Cor. 13:8), and Paul's love exemplified this. He was also like a faithful father (1 Thess. 2:9–19). Paul was a tent maker, and he earmarked some of the funds he needed for his ministry. When Paul had left Thessalonica, he was concerned about the church and sent Timothy back to see how things were going and to encourage the saints (ch. 3). Paul always prayed for the churches, and so should we. In 4:1–8, Paul warned the church to avoid the various forms of immorality that pervaded society in those days and are still with us today. Brotherly love is what he encouraged (3:9–12).

Several people in the Thessalonian church were grieving because some of their number had died, so Paul reminded them of the Lord's return (4:13—5:11). Knowing they would see Jesus, friends, and loved ones would bring peace and comfort to their hearts. We don't know when Jesus is coming, but the fact that He is coming again should give us a living hope. We should start each day as we wake up by saying, "Maybe today!" And we should live each day motivated by that promise. "Therefore comfort each other and edify one another" (5:11) are two very important "one another" statements in God's Word. We must be aware of others—their needs as well as their achievements—and be ready to encourage them.

Paul closed his letter with several important admonitions, some personal requests, and a benediction. He emphasized God's faithfulness to care for His people (5:24). God is faithful to forgive us our sins when we confess them (1 John 1:9), to chasten us (Ps. 119:75), to deliver us (1 Cor. 10:13), to sympathize with us and our needs (Heb. 2:17–18; 4:14–16), and to keep His Word (Heb. 10:23).

Second Thessalonians

In Paul's first letter to the Thessalonians, each chapter ends with a reference to Jesus Christ's return (1:10; 2:19; 3:13; 4:13–18;

5:23). The believers were discussing their interpretations of this important doctrine but disagreed in their application. We see this because some of them had quit their jobs and become idle watchers for the Lord's return (2 Thess. 3:6–15). Any interpretations of Bible doctrines that make us disobey clear Bible commandments are false interpretations and must be rejected. "I don't witness," a man told me, "because God knows who His elect are and will save them without my help." He forgot that the same God who ordains the end (saving lost sinners) also ordains the means to the end, *and we who are born-again believers are that means*! Read Matthew 28:16–20 and Acts 1:8. The traps Paul warned the Thessalonians about can still ensnare us today.

Knowing that one day we shall see Jesus and that our works will be judged, we ought to faithfully walk with the Lord, study and obey God's Word, pray, witness, and give of what we have to the Lord's work. Our confidence of the future should make us better sons and daughters, better parents, better neighbors, better servants of the Lord, better employees, and better citizens. I'm sure you agree. Paul clearly stated that Satan today attacks the church with lies and the influence of counterfeit Christians. There are even counterfeit ministers (2 Cor. 11:13–16, 26) who teach false doctrines along with a false gospel (1 Tim. 4:1; Gal. 1:6–7). Not every fellowship that calls itself a church really is a church. Some are "a synagogue of Satan" (Rev. 2:9). One day the "man of sin," the "lawless one," will arise; the Antichrist who, energized by Satan, will become a world ruler. The prefix *anti-* means both "against" and "instead of—counterfeit." (As a side note, I personally am convinced that believers will be taken to heaven before the rise of Antichrist.) We must beware of false teaching and grow in our knowledge of our Lord Jesus Christ, as Paul strongly encouraged.

The phrase "Lord Jesus Christ" is used eleven times in 2 Thessalonians, for Paul always exalted the Savior; and the phrase "as you know," or something similar, was used nine times in his first letter to them (1:5; 2:1, 5, 10–11; 3:3–4; 4:2; 5:2). Paul was reminding his readers that he had taught them, and if they were ignorant of what he was writing, it wasn't his fault. Paul was saying in 2 Thessalonians, "Christ is coming" (ch. 1) and "the lawless one" will be coming (2:1–12), "so stay steadfast in your faith" (2:13—3:15).

First Timothy

First and Second Timothy and Titus are known as "the pastoral epistles" because Paul wrote to men who were establishing and leading local churches. The theme for all three is given in 1 Timothy 3:15: "I write so that you may know how you ought to conduct yourself in the house of God." Paul could have called the three letters "order in the church!" The word *godliness* is used ten times in the pastorals, for a church becomes godly as the Lord works in and through godly people.

On Paul's second missionary journey, he met Timothy in Lystra, where the young man had a very good reputation as a believer. Paul "adopted" and mentored him, and he became a valuable helper in Paul's ministry. Timothy had a Jewish mother (Eunice) and grandmother (Lois) and a Greek father (Acts 16:1–5). Since Paul was God's special missionary to the Gentiles, and Paul himself was a Jew, Timothy's ancestry was an asset to the ministry.

What a privilege it was for Timothy to travel with Paul and learn from him, just as it's a privilege today for younger believers to learn from their elders who take time to mentor them. I thank the Lord for the opportunities He has given me to mentor young men and women who today are either in training for ministry or already in service. Paul and Timothy both took 2 Timothy 2:2 seriously, and so should we. Stop now to read the verse, and take it to heart. Churches today need more people who will take the time to mentor the coming generations.

Here is a brief outline of 1 Timothy:

1. Ministry of God's law and grace (1)
2. Ministry and leadership (2—3)
3. Ministry and apostasy (4)
4. Ministry and the church family (5:1—6:2)
5. Ministry and money (6:3–19)

In this book, Paul confronted a problem we still face today. There were people who tried to maintain the old covenant with the new covenant that every believer has in Christ (more about this when we get to Hebrews). We call them "Judaizers," or "legalists." They claimed to find deep truths in "fables and endless genealogies." As we learned from Galatians 3:24, the law was not written to save the righteous but to convict the unrighteous and bring them to Jesus. The law is our tutor to bring us to Christ. The sinners Paul mentioned have been in human society a long time and are with us today. Paul had left Timothy in Ephesus to deal with these false teachers and keep them from dividing the church and minimizing the gospel of God's grace. Paul's personal testimony in chapter 1 verses 12 through 20 was enough to refute the false teachers. If anyone was a lost legalist, it was Saul of Tarsus, the persecutor of the church!

Paul wasn't just giving Timothy good advice; he was declaring war on the false teachers (vv. 18–20). In the Greek language, the word *charge* is a military term that means "to give strict orders that must be obeyed" (1:3, 5, 18; 4:11; 5:7; 6:13, 17). It's obvious that some churches in Timothy's sphere of ministry were following unqualified leaders and believing unbiblical theology, and Timothy had to "clean house." We preach the grace of God, and we encourage leaders and teachers to focus on that grace.

The pastoral epistles give us the qualifications for holding office in the local church, and they were given for us to obey. I have sat on many a church nomination committee and have heard strange things from supposedly godly people. "Let's nominate Frank. He doesn't attend church faithfully and maybe holding an office would change that." Ouch! Better to leave the office vacant than to fill it with an unfaithful church member. Chapters 2 and 3 tell us clearly that those who fill church offices must be the best of the flock.

Paul pictured the church as a family ("the house of God," 3:15) in which the pastor sees the younger men as brothers, the younger women as sisters, the older men as fathers, and the older women as mothers. No family is perfect, but love accepts people (1:5), prays for them, and encourages them to mature in the faith. In Christ, we belong to each other, we need each other, and we serve each other. The leaders must make sure that the pure doctrine of God's grace is preached and taught (1:20; 2:7, 12; 3:2; 4:1, 6, 13, 16;

5:14; 6:1–3). Paul used the phrase "sound doctrine," which means "healthy doctrine" (1 Tim. 1:10; 2 Tim. 1:7, 13; 4:3; Titus 1:9, 13; 2:1, 2, 8).

In the final chapter, Paul dealt with a problem that has caused much trouble in the lives of God's servants—the love of money. God's servants have not always been adequately supported by the congregation, and this sometimes creates painful problems. Pastors have families to support, and if they are faithful in their ministry, they should be adequately supported (1 Tim. 5:17–18). "Double honor" can be translated "twice as much salary." But God's servants aren't the only people tempted by money, for church members commit the same sin (Acts 5:1–11).

Paul's final words to Timothy reveal the dangers we must confront in ministry: "O Timothy! Guard what was committed to your trust" (6:20–21). We are stewards of God's Word, and the enemy would like to rob us of that. To lose focus on the Word of God is to empty the ministry of power and truth.

It's worth noting that Paul cautioned Timothy against being oversensitive (2 Tim. 1:4), timid (vv. 7–8), and inattentive to his health (1 Tim 5:23).

Second Timothy

I don't know how many letters I have written during these many years of ministry. As far as we know, 2 Timothy was Paul's last inspired letter, sent to his beloved co-laborer Timothy, his "true son in the faith" (1 Tim. 1:2) and his "beloved son" (2 Tim. 1:2). Paul filled this letter with admonitions relating to Timothy's ministry, for Paul was more concerned with the future of the churches than he was his own life. He was "ready to be offered," (see 4:6) for he knew he was going to meet the Lord in heaven. He saw his death as the pouring out of a drink offering to the glory of God. Let's consider some of the admonitions he wrote to Timothy and apply them to our own lives and ministries.

Stir Up Your Gift and Hold Fast to Sound Words

When Timothy devoted himself to the ministry of the Word of God, the Lord gave him the spiritual gifts he needed for the work God had for him to do. How important it is that we walk with the Lord daily and keep our gifts in working order! This means spending time in the Word of God and being filled with the Spirit of God. Paul had written in his first letter, "Do not neglect the gift that is in you" (1 Tim. 4:14). Now he added, "Stir up the gift of God which is in you through the laying on of my hands" (2 Tim. 1:6). The Holy Spirit does not leave us when we fail (John 14:16), but He cannot fill us, empower us, and use us if we neglect our spiritual lives. Sometimes, the Lord must put us into difficult circumstances so we will realize how much we need to be stirred up! With the Spirit's help, we must "hold fast" to what the Lord has given us and use our gifts to glorify Him, build the church, and extend the kingdom. We must feed on "healthy words" and not permit lies to infect our system. We see an example of this in 1 and 2 Timothy. The Lord gave the living, healthy words to Paul (1 Tim. 1:11), and Paul gave them to Timothy (v. 18) and told him to guard them (6:20). Timothy was to give these words to others

(2 Tim. 2:2), and the blessed result is that the church grows in holiness and power.

Be Strong and Be Diligent

The grace of God is the source of the believer's power. We may feel weak and inadequate, but our weakness becomes strength if we are trusting in the Lord—"My grace is sufficient for you" (2 Cor. 12:9). Note that Paul compares God's people to soldiers (2 Tim. 2:3–4) and athletes (v. 5), and both demand discipline and determination. Conquering soldiers and winning athletes give themselves to their calling and willingly accept discipline and hardship, and so must God's people. Paul also compares us to farmers who must sow the seed into prepared soil, care for it, and know when to reap the harvest. Farmers also need patience (James 5:7), as do soldiers and athletes.

Turn Away!

Paul wrote this letter centuries ago, yet his description of the apostates (those who turn from the true faith) is quite contemporary. God's servants must not jeopardize their testimony by being influenced by apostate professed believers. Apostates have a form of godliness but have no connection with divine power. Take time now to read 2 Corinthians 6:14—7:1, and ask the Lord to give you wisdom and strength to obey. The emphasis in the local church must be on the doctrines given by the Lord and preached by the early church. There are people always seeking "some new thing" (Acts 17:21) who fail to hold on to the fundamental doctrines of the Christian faith. "Forever, O Lord, Your word is settled in heaven" (Ps. 119:89).

Be Watchful

The day is here when congregations have no appetite for the Word of God. They seem to want carnal entertainment rather than spiritual enlightenment and enrichment. Keep your eyes open! Satan is a counterfeiter and knows how to plant fake Christians in solid evangelical churches. God's people must obey what Paul commanded in 2 Timothy 4:1–5 and stay focused on sound doctrine.

Paul's "farewell speech" in 4:6–8 is a masterful expression of separation in the believer's life. We are not obligated to "fellowship" with every professed Christian. We need not become enemies, but we must be careful to maintain a clear testimony lest we lead others astray by our compromise. The Lord has a ministry designed for each of us, and we must fulfill that ministry. It is possible to speak the truth in love (Eph. 4:15) even as our Lord spoke to those who hated Him.

The Lord wants us to be good ministers of Jesus Christ (1 Tim. 4:6), no matter what vocation we have chosen. Paul pointed this out to Timothy in his first letter. A good servant of Jesus Christ will have a good conscience (1:5), fight a good warfare (1:18), pray for others (2:1–3), desire good works (3:1), and maintain a good testimony (3:7). We should be good soldiers of Jesus Christ (2 Tim. 2:3) and fight a good fight against the enemy (4:7–8).

Paul and his young associate could have struggled with a "generation gap" and created all sorts of problems, but they worked harmoniously and happily. It's been a great experience to serve the Lord together with younger men and women, and God has blessed us. I wish that every mature believer could mentor the younger generation as Paul commanded in 2 Timothy 2:2. What a difference that would make in families and churches!

Titus

For biographical data on Titus, read 1:1–5 and 3:12–15, plus 2 Corinthians 2:13 and 7:13–16, Galatians 2:3, and 2 Timothy 4:10. These verses indicate that Paul had led Titus to Christ, trained him, and sent him to minister in some difficult situations. You will find that Paul gave the same instructions and admonitions to Titus that he wrote to Timothy. In 1:5–9, Paul instructed Titus to appoint elders to direct the work of the church, and in 1:10–16, he instructed him to deal with the troublemakers in the church. Notice that church officers do not *hold* an office or *fill* it but *use it to serve the Lord and His people*. In 2:1–10, Paul cautioned Titus to preach sound, "healthy" doctrine to men and women, old and young, and make sure no false teachers crept into the church.

Verses 11–15 in chapter 2 are very important because they emphasize the grace of God. Nobody can be saved apart from the grace of God; nor can anyone serve the Lord without His grace. Grace not only brings salvation; it gives us the wisdom and knowledge we need to serve the Lord and help His people mature in the faith. Titus 1:9 and 2:1 stress the preaching of sound doctrine, and this means spiritual enrichment and not religious entertainment. *The leaders are to encourage spiritual growth by being examples* (2:7–8).

When I was a young pastor, the example of the experienced ministers in our city encouraged me tremendously.

Paul wisely advised us to treat the church members according to their needs as members of the church family. Some people might be critical, but you should treat them as if they were your own family and love them and listen to them (1 Tim. 5:1–2). Newer Christians may have a lot to learn, but supporting their imaginative yet godly ideas might usher a fresh sense of God's work. First Timothy 4:12 clearly states: "Let no one despise your youth, but be an example to the believers in word, in conduct, in love, in spirit, in faith, in purity." We need God's grace working in our own hearts to be able to deal with the problems (and problem people) that are a part of every local church. We must take Paul's words about grace (Titus 2:11—3:11) seriously and let the grace of God teach us to build and strengthen the people of God.

Paul's final words (3:12–15) tell us that he had several associates who assisted him in the ministry in different places. Paul was not a loner; he believed in teamwork. Paul didn't issue orders and insist on his own plans. He sought God's will, he had basic principles of ministry that he would not change, and he worked together with his fellow servants. He depended on the Lord, he recognized and appreciated the assistance of others, and he gave the Lord all the glory.

Philemon

The apostle Paul was a prisoner in Rome when he wrote the letter to Philemon, but the roles he played in the particular event he related are most interesting. Paul knew how to utilize every opportunity to win the lost and encourage the saved. First, we meet *Paul the soul-winner*, who had led Philemon, his wife, and his son to faith in Jesus Christ. This resulted in their starting a church in their house (v. 2). We get the impression that Philemon was well-off and had assisted Paul in the past. Onesimus, one of Philemon's slaves, had robbed his master and fled to Rome. In the Lord's providence, Onesimus ("profitable") met Paul in prison, and Paul led him to faith in Christ.

This leads us to *Paul the intercessor.* God had brought Paul and Onesimus together, but it appears that both men expected to be released soon (vv. 12, 22). Paul considered Philemon his "partner" in ministry (v. 17) and expected him to be concerned for the welfare of his disobedient slave, now a child of God. Being an apostle of the Lord, Paul could have commanded his friend Philemon, but he preferred to appeal to him in love (vv. 8–9). He asked his friend to receive Onesimus and forgive him for what he had done. Paul set a good example here for all of us to follow. Remember Jesus and the woman taken in adultery? He said to her, "Neither do I condemn you; go and sin no more" (John 8:11). Never underestimate the power of prayer and personal forgiveness.

But there is more, for we have *Paul the insurer.* He made it clear to Philemon that, if Onesimus owed him anything, Paul would pay the debt (vv. 17–20). Note that Paul wrote this letter personally, so it was like a promissory note that guaranteed payment. This reminds us of our Lord Jesus Christ's relationship to us in salvation: God the Father put the guilt of our sins on His Son when Jesus died for us on the cross. The Father credited it to His account! Each time we observe the Lord's Supper, we are being reminded that we are too poor to pay the price of our salvation but that Jesus paid it for us! Take time to read carefully Isaiah 53:4–6, and thank the Lord for paying our debt.

Paul didn't consider Onesimus just another convert because, in verse 10, he called him "my son Onesimus, whom I have begotten." Because of his faith in Jesus, Onesimus went from a slave to a beloved brother in Christ. Hallelujah, what a Savior!

ADVENTURE ASSIGNMENT #18

Select a portion of a chapter from one of the books we just covered and, using a reference Bible or the *New Treasury of Scripture Knowledge,* trace the cross references. See how the different verses contribute to a better understanding of your chosen text.

Chapter 19

Letters Especially to Jewish Believers

Hebrews and James

We must never forget that the first believers were Jews, and their missionary ministry took the message of the gospel to the Gentiles (Acts 2, 10—11, 15). A knowledge of the Pentateuch is a key to understanding the book of Hebrews. Keep in mind that the epistle to the Hebrews tells us what Jesus is doing now in heaven as He ministers to His church. Master the book of Hebrews and the Lord will have an easier time mastering your life.

Hebrews

"The Book of Hebrews was written to the Hebrews to tell them to quit being Hebrews."

Years ago, I heard Dr. Donald Grey Barnhouse make that statement, and I have never forgotten it. As the early church grew in number, both Jews and Gentiles were in the membership. The Gentiles had nothing to lose except their idols and a confusion of religious lies, but the Jews had centuries of history behind them: a temple and a priesthood in Jerusalem, a system of sacrifices, and a calendar of religious events that controlled religious life. The Jewish believers were helping write New Testament history, but some of them didn't quite know what to do with the Old Testament.

However, believers today, both Jews and Gentiles, have a complete Bible and can learn that the Old Testament prepares the way for the New Testament and sheds great light on the life of Jesus, the theology of the apostles, and the ministry of the church. The Jews boasted of their physical birth ("Abraham is our father") while the believers experienced a spiritual rebirth. Israel has an earthly inheritance, but Christians have a spiritual inheritance. Israel *had* a priesthood, but every believer *is* a priest (Rev. 1:6). The Jews offered many sacrifices day after day, but our Lord offered "one sacrifice for sins forever" (Heb. 10:12). A veil hung between the Jewish worshippers and the Lord, but when Jesus offered Himself on the cross, that veil was torn from top to bottom. This means we have access to the Lord through our risen and glorified Savior.

In every way, the Christian believer's position is superior to that of the most religious Jew. At least thirteen times in Hebrews, you will find the word *better* (or *superior*), for Hebrews was written to convince the readers that the Christian life was far superior to the Jewish life or the life that attempts to mingle Christianity with Judaism. The writer of Hebrews proved that Jesus is superior to the angels (1:4). He offers a superior hope (7:19) and gives us a superior covenant (7:22) with superior promises (8:6). He offered Himself as a superior sacrifice (9:22) and promises His people life in a superior country (11:16). The old covenant priests and Levites offered identical sacrifices day after day because animal blood cannot atone for human sin. But our Lord's one sacrifice for sin at Calvary settled the matter forever.

The book of Hebrews is filled with several challenging themes, such as the "let us" statements in chapter 4: "let us fear" (4:1–5); let us understand (see 4:6–10); let us be diligent (4:11–13); "let us hold fast" (4:14–15); and "let us … come boldly" (4:16). Chapter 8 explains the superiority of the new covenant, which I touched on earlier. It is ministered by a superior high priest (vv. 1–2) in a superior sanctuary (vv. 3–5) and is based on superior promises (vv. 6–13). How is the heavenly sanctuary superior? Chapter 9 tells us. The earthly sanctuary was made by man, but God made the heavenly sanctuary that was the pattern for the tabernacle on earth (v. 9). The blood of Jesus presented in the heavenly sanctuary dealt effectively with sin and gives cleansing, while in the earthly sanctuary sin was covered by an animal's blood (9:12–15). Additionally, what was limited to Israel is now available to the whole world (John 1:29).

Hebrews 8:5 reminds believers that they relate to that which is heavenly; therefore, they should set their affection and attention on things above (Col. 3:2). We have a heavenly calling (Heb. 3:1; 8:5) and have tasted of the heavenly gift (6:4). Our destiny is a heavenly country (11:16) because we have a heavenly citizenship (Phil. 3:20; Luke 10:20), and we will receive a heavenly inheritance (1 Pet. 1:4). This is part of our heavenly hope (Col. 1:5).

Hebrews reveals that Jesus is in heaven today with the Father, but what is He doing? For one thing, *He is speaking to His people through His Word* (Heb. 1:1–2:3; 12:25). He is helping us know His will and is guiding us so we know how to obey Him for His glory. Paul said of the Lord, "See that you do not refuse Him who speaks" (12:25). It isn't only the pastor and the Sunday school teachers who must hear His Word, but each believer must spend time daily in the inspired Word of God. Many voices demand our attention these days, but the most important is that of Jesus, as the Spirit teaches us from the Bible.

Our Lord is also *sustaining and upholding all things* (Heb. 1:3). He holds everything up so it won't fall and holds everything together so it won't come apart (Col. 1:17). He brings everything along on the right path at the right time so that it reaches His appointed goal. Following the current news, we sometimes feel that the Lord isn't at work or perhaps is not answering prayer, but such thinking is foolish and dangerous. (The next time you start questioning what the Lord is doing, take time to read Ps. 46.)

Jesus is speaking and upholding, but He is also *sitting* (Heb. 1:3). Where? On a throne in heaven (Isa. 6:1; Rev. 3:21). His work of redemption is ended, and He is now building His church and working in and through His people to accomplish His purposes on earth. Hebrews 2:10 tells us He is "bringing many sons to glory." No matter what the enemy may do, none of His sheep will be lost (see 1 Pet. 5:10 and John 10:27–29). We may experience suffering and disappointment, but He will stay with us to care for us and help us do His will. This leads us to the fact that Jesus is *sympathizing with his people* (Heb. 4:14–16). Because our Lord had a human body and lived with people and knew their pains and problems, He was (and is) able to encourage them and heal them.

Jesus is also *waiting expectantly* (10:11–14; Ps. 110:1–2). At the right time, He will return, come for His church, and ultimately defeat His enemies and establish His kingdom. I must confess that impatience is one of my personal weaknesses; I want things to happen now! But our Lord has been waiting for centuries. However, as He waits, He is *preparing*. He's preparing a city and a home for His people (11:16; John 14:1–6). He is equipping us for the ministry we will have in the world to come (Heb. 13:20–21). What that ministry is and how we will handle it depends on our service to the Lord today.

Finally, the Lord is *saving sinners and praying for the saints* (7:25). We can turn to Him in faith and receive the grace we need, and we can pray that the seed we have planted will bear fruit. Our work down here now depends on our faith and faithfulness, and our greatest desire should be to glorify the Lord.

In the early years of the church, some of the Jewish people didn't want to abandon their ancient faith and turn to Christ because they thought they were losing too much, when actually they would be gaining, for Jesus Christ would be their unchanging High Priest (4:14–16). Not only do we have a High Priest, but "we have … an anchor" which is *hope* (6:13–20). We also have an altar (13:9–10) where we can give acceptable sacrifices to the Lord. That altar is Jesus Christ, for it is "by Him" that we offer sacrifices (13:15–16). This would include our sacrifices of praise (13:15), of good works (13:16), of our bodies (Rom. 12:1–2), and of the money and other material things needed for the Lord's work (Phil. 4:18). We have a city (Heb. 13:14) and will dwell there and serve the Lord forever. Whatever we may lose because we are following

Jesus Christ, it will be more than compensated for by what He gives to us in return for all eternity.

Keep in mind that the epistle to the Hebrews is part of the "team" of Bible books that quote Habakkuk 2:4: "The just shall live by his faith" (see Heb. 10:38; Gal. 3:11; and Rom. 1:17). While we are on the subject of repetition, note three strategic "without" verses in Hebrews: "without shedding of blood there is no remission" (9:22); "without faith it is impossible to please Him" (11:6); and "holiness, without which no one will see the Lord" (12:14).

James

James was the "bishop" of the church in Jerusalem (Acts 12:17; 21:18) and a half-brother to Jesus (Matt. 13:55; Mark 6:3; Gal. 1:19). Before our Lord's death and resurrection, James and his brothers were unbelievers (John 7:1–5), but they did come to the faith. James sent his letter to Jewish believers "scattered abroad" who were experiencing trials and needed some errors corrected. The word *brethren* is used nineteen times. Here is a simple outline of the letter:

1. Temptations and trials (1:1–18)
2. Doers of God's Word (1:19–27)
3. Basic theology (2)
4. The tongue (3)
5. Admonitions (4—5)

The Christian life is not easy. We experience testing around us and temptations within us, and we must fight the world, the flesh, and the devil. One of the weapons James suggests we learn to use is *joy*. We should rejoice that we are being tested because that testing is proof that we're really born again. Not only that, but uncomfortable trials help us to build character (Rom. 5:1–5). I must admit that I have to battle impatience, but the only way to overcome impatience is to be tested and forced to wait. There are no impatience pills. The word *perfect* means "mature, under control." If we turn our circumstances over to the Lord, the Holy Spirit will help us get the victory. If I don't surrender my mind to the Lord and let Him take over, I will find myself unstable and therefore unable. Our desire in life must be to glorify God and not just to please ourselves. God may permit us to be tempted, and He may test us, but He also permits us to trust Him for victory *if we turn to Him.*

Satan may use our desire for wealth as bait to lead us astray. The hunger in our hearts feeds our desires and tempts us to disobey the Lord. If we aren't careful, we will start tempting ourselves! God always gives His children good gifts, while Satan gives what seems to be good but ends up being bad. The same Word of God that gives us our spiritual birth also enables us to defeat the enemy when he tempts us. When Satan tempted Jesus, the Lord defeated him with three verses from Deuteronomy. "Your word I have hidden in my heart, that I might not sin against You" (Ps. 119:11). The Word of God is a weapon Satan cannot overcome, but our responsibility is to know it, obey it, and trust it. James admonished us in verses 19 and 20 of chapter 1 to receive the Word, not to lose our temper, and not to talk too much.

Chapter 2 points us to the Son of God (vv. 1–4), the grace of God (vv. 5–7), the Word of God (vv. 8–11), and the judgment of

God (vv. 12–13). All of these are necessary if we are to mature in the faith and serve the Lord for His glory. James warned us that our speaking about God is no substitute for our hearing God's Word and obeying God's will (2:14–26). Living faith results in faithful living, but "faith without works is dead" (v. 26). If the Spirit dwells within us, then we must obey what God commands: "Let your light so shine before men, that they may see your good works and glorify your Father in heaven" (Matt. 5:16). If our walk isn't consistent with our talk, will anybody believe what we say?

In chapter 4, James warned us of four sins that we might commit but not even recognize. The first is *selfishness* (vv. 1–4). In my years of ministry, I have seen staff people and church officers just about split the church because they wanted their own way. If I'm at war with God in my heart and I can't honestly pray, "Thy will be done," then I'm going to start destroying the work of God. Selfish praying isn't prayer at all, and it won't bring God's blessing. *Worldliness* is the next of James' warnings (vv. 4–5). God's people must be separated from the world. If we become friendly with the worldly life (v. 4), our next step will be to love the world (1 John 2:15–17) and decrease our love for the Lord. The world will then leave its spots on us (James 1:27), which leads to being conformed to the world (Rom. 12:1–2). All of this could lead to being condemned with the world (1 Cor. 11:32).

Note the sins that follow: stubbornness (James 4: 6–7), carelessness (v. 8), and bitterness (vv. 11–17). In chapter 5, James warns us about living for pleasure (vv. 1–6), being impatient (vv. 7–12), and losing power in our prayer life (vv. 14–20). If we turn these negatives into positives (living for God, patience, and empowered prayer), we will enjoy victory! One of the keys to spiritual victory is a daily habit of looking into the Word of God. James compares it to a mirror for examination (1:22–26). Did you know that the laver in the Old Testament tabernacle was made out of the brass mirrors of the Jewish women? (Exod. 38:8). The laver was for restoration, enabling the priests to wash their hands and feet and be clean before the Lord. When I read and meditate on the God's Word, it's like taking a bath or a shower (Eph. 5:25–26). But the "mirror" of the Word is not only for examination and restoration; it is also for transformation. If you want a shining face, ponder Exodus 34:29–33 and 2 Corinthians 3:7–18 and put what you learn into practice.

ADVENTURE ASSIGNMENT #19

First, reconsider the "superior" statements in Hebrews. Think about how these passages can inspire you to choose not only a better way but the best way. Then look at the four kinds of sin mentioned in James 4. Consider how James offers a superior way that involves shunning those sins.

Chapter 20

The Last Words
of the Apostles

First Peter to Revelation

The inspired words of the apostles Peter, John, and Jude (our Lord's half-brother) bring the Bible to a close, and John warns us that nothing should be taken from the Word of God or added to it (Rev. 22:18–19). Translations come and go not because the Bible changes but because languages change. Old words take on new meanings and new words are added to our vocabulary by the thousands, year after year. "Forever, O Lord, Your word is settled in heaven" (Ps. 119:89).

First Peter

"You will know the apostle Peter when you get to heaven," the young preacher said, "because he's the fellow with the foot-shaped mouth."

I felt like getting up and walking out. The preacher wasn't worthy to carry Peter's shoes let alone make fun of him. Along with his two epistles, think of how much we have in the gospels and the book of Acts because Peter wasn't afraid to speak up. He won thousands of people to Jesus Christ—and is still doing so—and he also laid down his life for Jesus. His two epistles reveal his love and concern for the people of God. In this first epistle, he aims to prepare God's people for the impending persecution that the Roman government would unleash (4:12–19); and in his second epistle, he warned the churches about the false teachers who were stealthily creeping into the congregations and causing trouble. Foot-shaped mouth indeed!

How do we prepare for opposition and persecution? Peter gave us five instructions to obey.

Being Sure of Your Salvation (1:1—2:10)

Persecution usually cleanses a congregation and separates the sheep from the goats. It strengthens the true believers and the rest grow weaker and afraid. Peter opened his letter (vv. 1–5) with theology because what we believe helps control how we behave. Mark the theology in this section and imagine how it would help you if the enemy were persecuting you. Words like *elect, foreknowledge, sanctification,* and *mercy* are more than words. They are keys that unlock the doors to the spiritual blessings that keep us going when the going is hard and even dangerous.

As followers of Jesus Christ, we have eternal life and "a living hope" (1:3). Please read this section of your Bible and see the theology the Holy Spirit directed Peter to write. Note the variety of names Peter gave to the Christian experience. He told us that trouble is coming to the church, but if we know who we are in Christ and what we have in Christ, we can face the enemy unafraid—even in the midst of persecution.

Maintaining a Godly Walk (2:11–15)

"We ought to obey God rather than men," Peter said to the Jewish court (Acts 5:29) when persecution was starting in Jerusalem. In his letter, Peter made it clear that we are to respect those in authority even if we disagree with them, but obedience to the Lord comes first. We are to obey the law unless in so doing we disobey the Lord. Peter presents Jesus Christ as the greatest example of obedience, an obedience culminating at Calvary, where He died for the sins of the world. Serving God involves sacrifice, and at times, we can't do God's will unless we are willing to pay a price. We must take up our cross and follow Jesus.

A godly walk in everyday life is a witness in itself. Sometimes it's misunderstood, but for the most part, it is a light shining in a dark world.

Maintaining a Godly Home (3:1–7)

A godly home, with nothing to hide, presents a powerful witness to the lost, many of whom may be struggling with uncooperative or rebellious children—or perhaps it's the parents who aren't cooperating. The word *submissive* (3:1) in this passage irritates some people, but husbands and wives submit to each other in various ways. I have a very poor sense of direction; in that area, I'm the weaker vessel. But my wife has a flawless sense of direction. We have been together in foreign countries, and she has always known which way to go. She used to be a bookkeeper and is efficient when it comes to financial matters, so she handles that in our home. We work together on these things, and depending on the matter at hand, we submit to each other's experience, training, and abilities. We always had a family devotional time each morning and prayed with the children each evening before they went to bed. A few times we needed extra prayer and discussion, but I can't recall that we ever had recurring problems that couldn't be solved.

I like the phrase "heirs together" in 3:7, for the Lord is the giver and the couple are the receivers of His blessing. This could also refer to the gift of children, for Psalm 127:3 reads, "Behold, children are a heritage from the LORD." But it goes much farther, for as husband and wife work together in building their family and home, they depend on the Lord more and more. "Heirs together" beautifully describes a Christian couple, walking with the Lord and leading their children.

Understanding Suffering (3:8—4:19)

Suffering in the life of the Christian is different from the sufferings of the average person, for the Lord is in control, and we can work with Him in experiencing spiritual growth and blessing. In the believer's life, suffering is one of the Lord's "tools" for molding us; removing personal weaknesses; and strengthening our faith, hope, and love. Read Hebrews 12 and see what God says about "chastening." A judge punishes a guilty criminal, but a loving parent chastens a disobedient child. Many times in church history the Lord used suffering to mature His people and to prepare them for greater service. James wrote, "My brethren, count it all joy when you fall into various trials" (James 1:2).

Why rejoice in trials? Because if we walk by faith, they will mature us and help us grow in faith and obedience. Joseph's years in prison turned a boy into a man, as did David's experiences when King Saul was pursuing him. If we deliberately sin against the Lord, we may reap a painful harvest, but if we are obeying the Lord and we find ourselves in trouble, this may be our Father's loving hand of chastening—helping us grow in grace and holiness.

Submitting to God's Will (5:1–14)

This closing chapter speaks especially to the church's spiritual leaders, what Peter calls "the shepherds of the flock." The sheep are safe and secure so long as they recognize the shepherd's voice and obey it. If they disobey, they are in danger. You don't drive sheep; you lead them—and leaders must be good examples. The Holy Spirit is willing to teach us God's will from God's Word, and we must be willing to obey.

When it comes to knowing and doing the will of God, Satan our enemy seeks to confuse us and take us off the right path. One of his chief weapons is pride. He convinces us that we are so mature that we need not consult God's Word or take time to pray or to seek wisdom from our elders. Peter advised, "Therefore humble yourselves under the mighty hand of God, that He may exalt you in due time" (1 Pet. 5:6). All of us have cares, and the Lord is willing to help us carry them, understand them, and ultimately remove them. Paul suffered a thorn in the flesh and asked God to remove it, but God did just the opposite! He turned Paul's weakness into strength (2 Cor. 12:7–10)!

The will of God is an expression of the love of God. "The counsel of the Lord stands forever, the plans of His heart to all generations" (Ps.

33:11). God plans for us like this because He loves us, and we obey because we love Him.

There are places in our modern world where Christians are being persecuted, imprisoned, and even killed. Even Christians in the United States have been arrested because they refused to obey laws that contradict God's laws. "We ought to obey God rather than men," Peter told the Jewish court (Acts 5:29), and he was correct. May God help us follow his example and the example of Jesus Christ our Lord.

Second Peter

In his first letter, Peter sought to encourage and prepare the scattered believers concerning the persecution that the Roman emperor was planning to release against the churches. But in his second letter, Peter warned the believers to have nothing to do with the false teachers who were infecting local assemblies with their heresies. Notice in 1:12–15, Peter knew his own time was short, just as Jesus had told him years before (John 21:15–19). Before he gave his life for the cause of Christ, he wanted to warn the churches about those counterfeit Christians. If you knew your life were about to end, what special messages would you want to give to your friends and loved ones? Peter's message can be summarized in three admonitions.

Be Diligent (1:1–21)

Whether they know it or not, careless Christians are working for the enemy and not for the Lord. Peter exhorts his readers to be diligent and to "grow up" in their spiritual life (vv. 1–4). When they were born again into God's family, they received "all things that pertain to life and godliness" through the power of God and had everything they needed to become mature Christians. It's easy to deceive children, but mature people can quickly detect a fraud. We have the Word of God before us and the Spirit of God within us to teach us. Verses 5 through 8 describe the maturing Christian and verse 9 the immature one. Careless Christians can't see and can't remember! It takes time and diligence to grow in grace and knowledge and get equipped to fight the enemy and win.

In verses 16 through 21, Peter reaffirms the trustworthiness of the Word of God, for God's Word is our basic manual of arms, and our weapon for spiritual warfare (Heb. 4:12; Eph. 6:10–20). Peter reminded his readers that he had lived and ministered with the Lord Jesus Christ and didn't get his facts second hand. He mentioned the rich experience he and James and John had on the mountain when Jesus was transfigured and the Father spoke from heaven (Matt. 17:1–13). And I can enjoy similar experiences. I can read my Bible and hear God speaking to me. The Spirit can reveal the glory of Jesus Christ. All the inspired writers of the Bible help us see and hear the truth of God's Word and obey what the Lord tells us to do.

Peter describes careless believers as short-sighted, blind, and forgetful (2 Pet. 1:9).

Be Delivered (2:1–22)

False teachers intend to take control of churches others have built and lead them astray, and the teachers of truth must guard themselves and protect these congregations. The heretics don't teach truth, nor do they respect God's servants, yet many people follow them (2:2). Often, the motive of these liars, of course, is to get money (v. 3). Unless the congregation is well-taught and submissive to their Lord and their leaders, the invaders might take over the church.

Peter knew his Old Testament Scriptures and pointed out that the Lord often defeated the liars and upheld His own faithful people. When the ancient world forgot the Lord and rebelled against the godly life He required, God sent the flood and saved eight people: Noah and his family. God rescued Lot and his two daughters from the wicked cities of Sodom and Gomorrah. The Lord knows His own faithful people and can protect them and deliver them. Peter didn't mince words when he described the false teachers (vv. 10–17). They may be smooth talkers and pleasant to talk to privately, but they still deceive and destroy lives, and God is able to deliver His servants from the power of the evil one. Read verses 12–22 carefully. Are you enraptured by false teachers—their radio and television programs, the books they write, the letters they send you? Then you need to be delivered!

Be Mindful and Beware! (3:1–18; see verses 2 and 17)

We must be mindful of the truths we have learned from the Scriptures and beware of the false teachers' deceptions lest we get trapped, start believing false doctrines, and tear down what the Lord wants built up. Bible-rejecting churches exist today that once were centers of evangelism, Bible teaching, worship, and wide ministry. It didn't happen overnight, but it happened, primarily because the true believers were not mindful of what was going on and opposing it. Beware! The same tragedy has occurred with schools that were once evangelical and sought to win the lost. Today they joke about evangelism, absolutes, and the devotional life. I recall one school that once had several godly presidents who taught and preached the Word of God. Then a president was chosen who was a chameleon—an evangelical when with evangelicals but a false teacher when he was not.

Be mindful and beware! The day of the Lord will arrive, and those who have abandoned the faith will face judgment. Let's instruct the next generations and prepare them to carry on the ministries of evangelism, church planting, Christian education, missions, and helping the needy. Peter warned us that professed Christians can "fall from [their] own steadfastness" (3:17) and deny the very teachings they once defended. How do we remain steadfast? Practice 2 Peter 3:18: "But grow in the grace and knowledge of our Lord and Savior Jesus Christ." And be sure He gets the glory!

The First Epistle of John

The apostle John didn't arrange his first epistle as neatly as he did his gospel. Reading this epistle is like walking up a circular staircase and meeting the same people at almost every turn. John wrote on about a dozen different topics, and each statement either emphasized an old truth or introduced a new truth. Led by the Spirit, he wrote as though he was holding up a large, beautiful diamond and was causing rays of sunlight to produce different shapes and colors. John wanted us to pause and ponder and not think we have already covered that topic and can move on.

Keep your Bible open, and I will give you the topics and references. Take time to read the verses, meditate on them, and compare them. I might make a comment or two, but the important thing is that you read the verses for each topic and think about what they say.

Life

John began by affirming that he had seen eternal life manifested in Jesus Christ (1:1–2; 2:25; 3:14–16; 5:11–13, 20). It was not a vision or a dream but a "hands-on" experience day after day. John wrote about reality. God had come to earth in living human form! "In the beginning was the Word" opens John's gospel and his statement in 1 John 1—2 parallels it. Jesus is the eternal Word, the living Word that imparts life to all who hear and believe. John opened and closed this letter with eternity. Think about it.

Fellowship

For three years, the apostles lived with Jesus, ate with Him, traveled with Him, watched Him minister, and listened to Him teach divine truth (1:3, 7). The word *fellowship* means "to have in common." Different kinds of people comprise the church, people who nevertheless have in common eternal life, the Holy Spirit within, and a home in heaven. They worship and work together to the Lord's praise and glory. John wrote his gospel so that sinners would believe and enter the fellowship (John 20:31), and he wrote this epistle so that saved sinners might enjoy and enlarge the fellowship. If we are walking in the light, we are in fellowship with the Lord and His people (1:5–7).

The word *abide* relates to this and is used in 1 John nineteen times and in John's gospel seventeen times. To abide in Christ means to fellowship with Him and do His will. Read John 15 for more on "abiding."

Joy

Why did John write this letter? So that we might have joy in our Christian life (1:4). Happiness comes primarily from happenings, but joy comes from the Lord as we fellowship with Him and serve others. Joy comes from the Spirit's work in our hearts, for "the fruit of the Spirit is love, joy ..." (Gal. 5:22). We find joy in God's Word as the Spirit teaches us, and we experience joy in fellowship with other Christians. We all have our difficulties and disappointments, but the Lord will give us joy even when our bodies and our circumstances seem to be against us.

Light

Light symbolizes several things in the Bible, including God (1:5; John 8:12), God's Word (Ps. 119:105), and God's people (Matt. 5:14–16). But light also can mean knowledge and truth while darkness can mean ignorance and lies (1 John 1:5–7; 2:8–11). John has much to say about truth (1:6, 8; 2:4, 21; 3:18–19; 4:6; 5:6). Check the "darkness" verses, too (1:5–6; 2:8–9, 11). Note also some of the people in Scripture who are identified with darkness, such as King Saul (1 Sam. 28), Samson (Judg. 16:21), and Judas (John 13:30).

Cleansing

Cleansing pictures the forgiveness of sins (1:7–10). David prayed to be made "whiter than snow" (Ps. 51:7), and in the upper room, Jesus washed His disciples' feet (John 13:1–17). Additionally, as we meditate on Scripture, the Word of God cleanses us (John 15:3; Eph. 5:26).

Overcoming Power

This means overcoming temptation (2:1–11, 14; 3:4–9). Jesus is our Advocate who represents us before the Father and forgives us when we confess our sins (1:9–10). As our High Priest, He also enables us to resist the world, the flesh, and the devil so that we do not sin.

Love

We are to love God and God's people, our neighbors, and our enemies (2:7–11; 3:16–23; 4:7—5:5). We are also to love God's Word (Ps. 119:97). John 3:16 tells us that God loves the world and gave His Son to save sinners, and 1 John 3:16 tells us we ought to lay down our lives in love for our brothers and sisters in Christ.

The Will of God

Make your choice: either the will of the world or the will of God (2:15–17). The will of God is an expression of the love of God (Ps. 33:11); the will of the world involves lust. Doing God's will involves humility and faith while doing the world's will requires pride and very high self-confidence. Pleasing the Lord is much easier than pleasing the world, and the consequences are eternal.

Knowledge

Because believers have God's Word, the Holy Spirit, and prayer, they have access to God's wisdom and the ability to understand what God wants them to do (2:18–29; 5:18–21). Many times in my ministry, I've struggled with a passage and gone to bed with no solution. But in the middle of the night, I've awakened and discovered the Lord teaching me! To take advantage of these occasions, I keep a lamp, a pen, and a tablet next to the bed so I can write down what the Lord teaches me. If I don't, I'll go back to sleep and forget the night school lesson! "My eyes are awake through the night watches, that I may meditate on Your word," wrote the psalmist (Ps. 119:148). The Lord will grant wisdom, even if it sometimes comes when we'd rather sleep. He warns us about the enemy and tells us what to do. He encourages us and sometimes rebukes us, but all of this is for our good. Note the phrase "we know" in this epistle.

Hope

Love and hope go together. Jesus loves His "little children" and wants them to live with Him forever (3:1–3). We have a "blessed hope" that our Lord will one day return and take His people home to heaven. If we believe His promise, it should motivate us to obey Him—John calls it "purifying ourselves"—and be ready when He comes.

Holy Spirit

When we obey our Lord, the indwelling Holy Spirit can work in us and through us and glorify the Lord Jesus (3:24—4:6; 5:6–10). (The Holy Spirit is mentioned often in John's gospel.) John warns his readers not to meddle with false teachers because they are controlled by the antichrist, but "the Spirit is truth" (5:6). The Spirit bears witness to us about Jesus so that we might bear witness to a lost world (Acts 1:8). "God is greater than our heart" (1 John 3:20), and the Holy Spirit can deliver us from thoughts and feelings that might lead us astray. The Spirit within us is greater than the spirits at work in our world. As we meditate on the Word of God, the Spirit bears witness to us and imparts the truth of God.

Prayer

What a privilege it is to "take it to the Lord in prayer" (5:14–17). If the Spirit leads us and we claim God's promises in the Scriptures, we can pray with confidence. The better we know the Lord and His Word, the more effective our praying will be. But if we know there is sin in our hearts, the Lord will not hear us (Ps. 66:18). The Spirit and the Word of God will convict us, and we must confess our sins (review 1 John 1:5–10).

There are other topics we could consider, but this selection gives you a good idea of the spiritual truths John offered us. Don't let the "circular staircase" of truths discourage you. Each time you read John's first epistle, you will see truths that you never saw before, so keep studying!

The Second Epistle of John

John didn't identify "the elect lady," but he did identify his theme— "the truth"—and described our responsibilities regarding God's truth. First, *we should love the truth* (1:3). It isn't enough for us simply to know God's Word or even respect it, but we must love the Word of the Lord. "Oh, how I love Your law! It is my meditation all the day" (Ps. 119:97, and see vv. 48, 113, 127, 159, 165, and 167). When we receive an email or a letter from someone we love, we drop everything and read it. If we truly love the Lord, we will love what He says to us. For years, I have set aside time at the beginning of each day to read the Scriptures, pray, and lay hold of the principles and promises the Lord wants me to know.

Our second responsibility is *to walk in the truth* (2 John 4–6). That means to obey it in every aspect of life. John emphasized the new commandment Jesus gave us that we love one another (John 13:31–35). To live motivated by love is to live as Jesus lived and to experience the blessings that the Holy Spirit wants to share with us.

Holding on to the truth is our third responsibility (2 John 7–11). The world around us does not believe in absolutes, and it knows how to manipulate lies and occasional truths. Remember the college student who said, "There are no absolutes"? If there truly aren't any, that would include the student's statement; the paradox there ends the conversation. During my lifetime, I have heard truth attacked, mangled, denied, laughed at, and cursed—yet the truth remains. *Don't let anybody rob you of the truth!* Obeying God's truth not only gives us wisdom and blessing, but it defeats the enemy and enables us to serve a needy world. John warns us to be cautious how we entertain people who deny God's truth lest we give others the impression we agree with them. Loving our unsaved friends and neighbors is one thing, but opening the door to cultists is quite another.

All of this leads us to the fourth responsibility: *enjoy the truth and share it* (vv. 12–13). It's enriching to spend time with Christian friends and interested unsaved friends discussing God's Word and applying it to our lives and ministries. It's good to read the truth and absorb it, and it's also good to discuss it and tell others what God's truth means in your own life. The apostle John wrote much that has blessed the world; we can learn from others, and they can learn from us. The best way to promote and defend the truth is to practice it in daily life.

The Third Epistle of John

This letter mentions three different people—Gaius, Diotrephes, and Demetrius—and we may learn something from each of them.

Gaius (vv. 1–8) was evidently converted under John's ministry, for John called him one of his spiritual children (v. 4). John was concerned about his friend's health and prayed that he might be as healthy physically as he was spiritually. Both should concern us when we intercede for others. Didn't Jesus and His disciples heal the sick and afflicted and feed the hungry? Gaius also helped support traveling evangelists who were devoted to the Lord and to sharing the truth. Those who go out to minister and those who serve at home by helping support them are both important "fellow workers for the truth" (v. 8).

I suppose almost every church has in the congregation a trouble-making dictator like Diotrephes (vv. 9–12). He did not respect John's authority as an apostle and put himself above everybody else in the congregation. He ignored a letter John had written to the church and insisted that he was first in leadership and had the final say-so in everything. He had to approve who could join the fellowship, and he thought he could even dismiss people from the church! How painfully sad and how destructive it is when a church has members like this! John made it clear that he would visit the church, confront Diotrephes personally, and set matters straight. Everything rises and falls with leadership, and if the leadership is proud and selfish, the church will not prosper.

On the other hand, in my own pastoral ministry, I've always been grateful for people like Demetrius who live godly lives and have good testimonies. We need more church members who are walking with the Lord and working with others to help the church grow in grace and in number. When Jesus washed His disciples' feet (John 13:10–17), He made it clear that we are to serve one another and not use one another to build our own "kingdom." If you want to know how to treat other people in the church, take time to find and read the "one another" statements in the New Testament.

The Epistle of Jude

Jude and James were half-brothers of Jesus (Matt. 13:55; Mark 6:3; Acts 15:22). Jude's epistle deals with the false teachers who were getting into the churches and leading people astray. Jude intended to write on a different theme but the Lord led him to warn the churches of this dangerous situation. His brief but powerful letter may be outlined as follows:

> Introduction (1–3)
> 1. What the false teachers do (4–11)
> 2. What the false teachers are (12–19)
> 3. What God's people must do (20–25)

What the False Teachers Do

They are not open and honest in their ministry but secretive, having "crept in unnoticed" into the churches under false pretenses (v. 4). They masquerade as devoted children of God when they are actually seeking to lead the church family into false doctrines. The apostle Peter issued the same warning in his letter as Jude does here (2 Pet. 2:1–3). The false teachers aimed to "turn the grace of God into lewdness" (Jude 4). In other words, they told the people that God's grace gives believers freedom to do as they please. Paul refuted this lie in Romans 6, and John dealt with it in 1 John 3:4–9. These false teachers denied that Jesus was God come in human flesh. They denied what John affirmed in his first epistle (2:18–23; 4:1–4). They did not believe God's Word or believe in God's Son, Jesus Christ.

In verses 5–7, Jude reached back into the Old Testament to show that the Lord judges those who commit such sins. God judged the people who refused to enter Canaan, and they wandered for forty years (1 Cor. 10; Heb. 3—4). He judged the angels who rebelled against God (2 Pet. 2:4–5); the wicked cities of Sodom and Gomorrah (v. 7; Gen. 18:16—19:29); and Cain, Baalam, and Korah as well. Cain was an unbeliever (Gen. 4), Baalam was greedy for wealth (Num. 22—24), and Korah would not submit to God's authority as vested in Moses (Num. 16). False teachers speak abusively and argue with the Lord (Jude 8–10). "It is a fearful thing to fall into the hands of the living God" (Heb. 10:31).

What the False Teachers Are

Jude listed ten characteristics of false teachers that make them very dangerous. They are blemishes on the body of Christ, even at the church love feasts. Peter used the same image (2 Pet. 2:13). Their evil doctrines and practices defile the church. They are selfish (Jude 12), serving themselves instead of serving their people. Jude's phrase "clouds without water" means they promise showers of blessing but have no refreshing water (Prov. 25:14). They are rootless and fruitless, twice dead! Wild waves are destructive, and wandering stars will lead the traveler astray; so will these teachers. False teachers are ungodly, unappreciative, and arrogant in their scoffing at those who are faithful to the Lord. Each of these images exposes the deception false teachers practice, and every believer must be alert and aware. They are not spiritual people but sensual, resulting in divisions in the church ("Are you for me or against me?"). Division weakens the church and opens the way for trouble.

What God's People (True Believers) Must Do

We must start with love. Jude called his readers "beloved" (vv. 3, 17, 20), an indication that he knew them. Start "building yourselves up on your most holy faith" (Jude 20), he first admonished because "love never fails"

(1 Cor. 13:8). As Paul wrote, "The fruit of the Spirit is love" (Gal. 5:22). Some people are wrong in their thinking because they are ignorant, or perhaps they have been taught by the wrong people. The more we grow in faith and knowledge, the better able we are to help others abandon false thinking and receive the truth.

Prayer in the Spirit is the next essential, asking the Lord to cleanse our minds and hearts and grant us spiritual wisdom and insight. Remember, we are fighting against Satan and his demonic forces, and prayer is one of our best weapons. Waiting patiently for the Lord to work in the minds and hearts of teachers and followers is important. As we watch and pray and wait and pray, the Lord will work in their hearts and ours. The Lord will give us discernment (Jude 22–23), and we will know what to say and do. Verses 24 and 25 are a benediction of blessing I have used for many years. We are not able to change people, but God will use what we say and do to transform them.

Revelation

The Holy Spirit used the apostle John to give us three different kinds of inspired literature: *the gospel of John*, where the emphasis is on *believing* (20:31), *the epistles of John*, with an emphasis on *behaving* (1 John 2:1), and *the Revelation of Jesus Christ by John*, where the emphasis is on *beholding* (The word *behold* is used twenty-six times). The Lord showed John one prophetic tableau after another, and we are invited to study them. What a privilege!

The persecution that both Peter and Jude wrote about did come, and John was sent as a prisoner to work in the mines on the island of Patmos. But the Lord can teach His children no matter where He places them, and He gave John remarkable visions of the future that still stir minds and hearts today. One of the key words in the book is *seven*, a number that carries the idea of completeness. As you examine this simple outline of the book, note that the events work together to bring God's plan to a successful conclusion. Our Lord is the beginning and the end, and what He starts He finishes.

1. Christ and the seven churches (1—3)
2. Christ opens the seven seals (4—8:1)
3. Angels blow the seven trumpets (8:2—11)
4. John beholds seven signs (12—14)
5. Angels empty seven bowls of wrath (15—16)
6. John beholds seven climactic events
   (17—22:5)
7. Final admonitions (22:6–21)

Please remember that this book is about Jesus Christ and not just about prophetic events. From beginning to end, Jesus is seen, is heard, and is glorified. Take time to get acquainted with the various names and titles of Christ in this fascinating book.

- Alpha and Omega (1:8, 11; 21:6; 22:13)
- Amen (3:14)
- Beginning of the Creation of God (3:14)
- Bright and Morning Star (22:16)
- Faithful Witness (1:5; 3:14; 19:11)

- First and Last (2:8)
- Firstborn from the Dead (1:5)
- King of the saints (15:3)
- King of Kings (17:14)
- Lamb (5:6)
- Lion of the Tribe of Judah (5:5)
- Lord (17:14)
- Morning Star (2:28; 22:16)
- Offspring of David (22:16)
- Reaper (14:15)
- Root of David (22:16)
- Witness (1:5; 3:14)
- Word of God (19:13)

It's also interesting to contrast *the Revelation* (the end of the Bible) with *Genesis* (the beginning of the Bible).

Genesis	The Revelation
The first creation (1:1)	New heaven and earth (21:1)
Satan's first attack (3:1–24)	Satan's last attack (20:7–10)
The sun shines (1:16)	No sun needed (21:23)
The sea created (1:10)	No more sea (21:1)
The serpent cursed (3:14–17)	No more curse (22:3)
Adam given a wife (2:18–23)	Marriage of the Lamb (19:6–9)
The serpent judged (3:15)	The serpent doomed (20:1–3)

The fact that the letters to the seven churches were first on the agenda (1:4–8; chs. 2—3) suggests that what the Lord revealed to

John was important to the ministry of the churches in that day. The churches in John's day were not unlike our churches today, and we would be wise to learn about them and examine our own ministries. Some of the churches were faithful and fruitful, but others tolerated sin and sinful people. The seven churches have been understood to represent seven stages in the history of the church, but even if so, the first application must be for us today. These churches existed at the same time and may in some ways illustrate religious history, but the first application must be to our own lives and ministries today. Read the letters to the churches carefully and apply them first to yourself and the church where you worship.

Looking further into this book, it's interesting that our Lord is identified with both a lion and a lamb (5:5–6). It's a paradox, for the two animals are quite opposite each other. The lion makes us think of a king and the lamb a sacrifice, but is not Jesus both? He was as gentle as the lamb led to the slaughter (Isa. 53:7) and as powerful and kingly as the lion.

You will want to note the seven beatitudes in the book of Revelation: 1:3; 14:13; 16:15; 19:9; 20:6; 22:7, 14; and you should mark the twenty-six times the Lamb is mentioned (5:6, 8, 12, 13; 6:1, 10, 16; 7:9–10, 14, 17; 12:11; 13:8; 17:14; 19:7, 10; 21:9, 14, 22–23, 27; 22:1, 3). Elsewhere in Scripture, Isaac asked his father, "Where is the lamb for a burnt offering?" (Gen. 22:7). John the Baptist answered the question: "Behold! The Lamb of God who takes away the sin of the world" (John 1:29). Back in Revelation, the huge heavenly choir exalted Him: "Worthy is the Lamb who was slain" (5:12). There are also four doxologies: 1:4–8; 4:11; 5:13;

and 7:12. To worship and praise the Lord is the chief occupation of the residents of heaven, as it should be.

Please note that the furnishings of the tabernacle and temple are mentioned in the Revelation: the brazen altar (6:9), the laver (4:6), the incense altar (8:3–5), the lamps (4:5), the cherubim (4:6–7), and the throne (4:2). The word *throne* is mentioned forty-seven times in the book; there is an emphasis on the majesty and regal ministry of the Savior.

There are a dozen references to the "earth dwellers," in other words, the people who live on the earth and for the world and who have not trusted the Savior (3:10; 6:10; 8:13; 11:2, 10; 12:12; 13:8, 12, 14; 17:2, 8). The followers of Jesus Christ are *in* this world to serve, but they are not *of* this world to sin. First John 2:15–17 settles that, and see John 17:12–19. The "earth dwellers" belong to Babylon, but the people of God belong to Jerusalem. It doesn't take much to understand why.

Definite patterns appear in The Revelation of Jesus Christ, but students don't all agree on what they teach us. Some see Jesus returning before the tribulation while others see a mid-tribulation rapture of the church or even a post-tribulation rapture. The important thing is not that I have an accurate calendar but that I am ready *today* for the Lord to return, faithfully doing what He has called me to do. The students of prophecy who have set dates have all been wrong. The believers who have set their hearts on waiting, watching, and working will be ready.

ADVENTURE ASSIGNMENT #20

We have covered a lot of territory. Has one book in this last section especially captured your interest—not because it's brief but because it offers you opportunities to learn and grow? Read it again and make your own outline. Make a list of the images and symbols it contains, and trace some of the cross-references to other books in the Bible. If you still have some energy, use your own outline of the book and decide how you would teach the book to a class.

Chapter 21

Gathering Up the Fragments that Remain

As you have read this book and done the assignments, you have probably asked some questions I haven't answered. I will try to remedy that in this final chapter.

> *How do I select a translation of the*
> *Bible that will meet my needs?*

The Bible you select for serious study must first of all have *an accurate text*. Many popular versions that are interesting to read can't always claim to be accurate. Years ago, Dr. A. W. Tozer published an essay titled "Confessions of a New Translation Addict" and pointed out that using a popular new translation is no guarantee you will discover new truths or become a capable student of the Bible.[1] I have known people who rush to purchase new versions only to discover that the new text didn't provide new understanding. Your Bible should have an adequate system of cross-references so you can connect the verses and let the Bible explain itself. My favorite study text is *The New American Standard Version.* My second choice is *The New King James Bible.* Years ago, a well-known Christian musician and speaker was given a modern translation by his publisher, and he asked me about it. "This book just doesn't seem to talk to me," he told me. You must choose the version that "talks to you" and *learn how to use it.*

Must I purchase a study Bible?

I was surprised to discover that I have fourteen different study Bibles in my library! Some were purchased, some were given to me by friends, and some were sent by their publishers. A study Bible combines the biblical text with a "digest" Bible dictionary so you have your resources all in one volume. The editors provide outlines and introductions for each book of the Bible, explanations of difficult passages, and diagrams and maps to illuminate the text. Study Bibles can be great time-savers, but they are not substitutes for Bible dictionaries, Bible encyclopedias, or more detailed books. And you don't need fourteen of them! The text of the Bible is the most important consideration. If you can afford to purchase a study Bible, by all means, do so. But don't sacrifice the text for the extras.

> *I like to read books and my Bible while taking the train into the city and home again five days a week. Is that the proper place to handle things spiritual?*

When I was a seminary student, I used to study my Greek and Hebrew vocabulary cards while on the train, which to me seemed a proper use of my time. If possible, while you are at home over the weekend, review in the privacy of your home what you have studied during the week. Beware of shortcuts. Whether on the train or in the station, give it your best.

What's involved in marking the Bible?
Is this practice a necessity?

Let me begin with an interesting piece of history. C. I. Scofield, then an attorney and a young believer, visited his friend C. E. Paxton and was shocked to find him marking a page in his Bible with an ink pen. "Man, you're spoiling that fine new Bible," he said, but Paxton explained that he was only connecting two verses: Acts 8:5 and 8:8. Read these verses in your Bible and discover the connection yourself. This experience eventually led to the publication of the *Scofield Reference Bible*, which is still a popular study Bible today. To begin with, the Bible you mark must be printed on sturdy paper that will take the ink you use, and your pen must have a fine point and contain an acid-free ink. You will find excellent fine-point pens with many colors of ink in an artist's supply store.

Why do we mark our Bibles? To permanently record the spiritual truths the Lord has taught us. Mr. Paxton in my story connected Acts 8:5 and 8:8 to show that receiving the gospel brings joy to people. If I were studying John 3, I would probably circle the word *must*, which appears four times in the chapter. Check it out for yourself and decide why. Marking the Bible must not be an impulsive, careless activity but a careful and deliberate one. To underline everything is to underline nothing and mess up a page. It would be better to draw a line or write a note in the margin. Over the years, I have often referred to the markings in my various Bibles as I have prepared sermons, lessons, and chapters for books.

How much time should I devote to serious Bible study?

It's not the length of the time so much as the depth of the encounter that makes the difference. As with your daily devotional time, spend enough time to learn and be spiritually refreshed. If study time is available, take advantage of it. Be neither a clock-watcher nor a time-waster. Many believers keep a study notebook into which they may record this adventure. Over the weeks, you will gradually discover and develop your own particular style.

I have problems with Bible names. Help me!

Most Bible names, especially the geographical names, give us trouble, but this is where a good Bible dictionary or a study Bible comes in handy. A name's meaning can be very important to the purpose of the narrative. When a person's name is changed, this is especially significant. You are right to pay attention to Bible names, both of people and places.

I sometimes learn things from my studies that excite me, and I want to share them with others. Do I have that privilege?

Sharing is permissible so long as we don't become nuisances or interject into the class ideas that don't relate to the topics at hand. The

Lord may be preparing you to encourage others who will come to you with their problems. Whatever we learn, we must first apply it to our own lives in private. Once we have done this, the Lord will give us opportunities to minister to others. From this may come an invitation to lead a Bible study group or simply to be available to counsel with folks. Don't promote yourself: be patient and let God work in His way and His time. Eventually our gifts will make room for us (Prov. 18:16).

*When two versions of the Bible differ radically
or two expositors differ, what should I do?*

Accept the fact that good and godly people may disagree, but you can still make your own decision and, if necessary, change it later. Weigh the facts carefully, pray for wisdom (James 1:5), and don't be afraid to say, "I don't know."

Notes

Chapter 4

1. Forsythe, P.T. *Positive Preaching and the Modern Mind.* (London: Independent Press, 1953), 28.

Chapter 5

1. Songwriter, "I Won't Have to Cross Jordan Alone," http://www.azlyrics.com /lyrics/johnnycash/iwonthavetocrossjordanalone.html.

2. Samuel Stennett, "On Jordan's Stormy Banks I Stand," cyberhymnal.com, http://www.cyberhymnal.org/htm/o/j/ojordsbi.htm.

3. Watchman Nee, *The Normal Christian Life* (Fort Washington, PA: CLC Publications, 2012), 97.

4. F. W. Robertson, *Sermons by the Reverend F. W. Robertson*, (Parish of Brighton Holy Trinity, 1864), 66.

5. George McDonald, //izquotes.com/quotes/?q=respectable+selfishness&t=1.

6. Lucille Ball, "Lucille Ball," goodreads.com, www.goodreads.com/quotes /15947-i-have-an-everyday-religion-that-works-for-me-love

Chapter 6

1. John. F. Kennedy, *Profiles in Courage* (New York: Harper & Brothers, 1955), 245.

Chapter 8

1. Alexander Whyte, (1836-1921).
2. Paul Johnson, *A History of the Jews*, (New York: Harper and Row, 1987), page 585-588.

Chapter 9

1. Winston Churchill, "The Few," churchillsocietylondon.org, www.churchill -society-london.org.uk/thefew.html.
2. William D. Longstaff, "Take Time to Be Holy," hymnary.org, http://hymnary .org/text/take_time_to_be_holy.

Chapter 10

1. Jennie Evelyn Hussey, "Lead Me to Calvary," hymnary.org, http://hymnary.org /text/king_of_my_life_i_crown_thee_now.

Chapter 13

1. Jeremy Taylor, "Jeremy Taylor Quotes," http://christian-quotes.ochristian.com /Jeremy-Taylor-Quotes/page-4.shtml.
2. Benjamin Franklin, www.azquotes.com/quote/650876.
3. Kittie L. Suffield, "God Is Still on the Throne," www.hymntime.com/tch/htm/g /i/s/gisontth.htm.

Chapter 16

1. G. Campbell Morgan, *The Great Physician* (London: Morgan & Scott Marshall Publications, 1972), 353.

Chapter 17

1. B. Metzger, "Jesus and Others and You," childrenschapel.org, http://childrenschapel.org/biblestories/sheetmusic/joysong.html.

Chapter 21

1. A.W. Tozer, "Confessions of a New Version Addict," http://www.orange-street -church.org/text/addict.htm.

BE TRANSFORMED

The *Transformation Study Bible* — a cover showing a tree silhouette with the title "The *Transformation* STUDY BIBLE" and the NLT logo.

Don't copy the behavior and customs of this world, but let God transform you into a new person by changing the way you think. Then you will learn to know God's will for you, which is good and pleasing and perfect. — Romans 12:2

The *Transformation Study Bible* pairs the rich and readable text of the New Living Translation with the wisdom of one of the world's most respected pastors. This unique doorway into Scripture will equip and inspire you to live more fully, to understand more deeply. To live a life transformed.

David C Cook
transforming lives together